GOD'S PROPHET, GOD'S SERVANT

A Study in Jeremiah and Isaiah 40–55

JOHN GOLDINGAY

THE PATERNOSTER PRESS
Carlisle UK

British Library Cataloguing in Publication Data

Goldingay, John
    God's Prophet, God's Servant: Study in
    Jeremiah and Isaiah 40–50. – New ed. –
    (Biblical Classics Library)
    I. Title II. Series
    224.06

    ISBN 0–85364–604–x

Typeset by Busby Typesetting and Design, Exeter
and Printed in the U.K. for The Paternoster Press,
P.O. Box 300, Carlisle, Cumbria, CA3 0QS
by Cox and Wyman Ltd, Reading

TO MY MOTHER
AND IN MEMORY
OF MY FATHER

Contents

Foreword

These studies of Jeremiah and Isaiah 40-55 arose from my teaching and preaching, whose contexts I am glad to recall: especially the congregation of Christ Church, Chilwell, the summer houseparty of the Church's Ministry among the Jews at High Leigh, and most of all the students and staff of St. John's College, Nottingham. I am grateful to Mrs Patti Boyland and Mrs Janet Gillard for their beautiful typing from my much emended handwriting.

I have occasionally explicitly quoted from works on these two prophets, or on the Old Testament more generally, and I am, of course, much more indebted to such works than a mere occasional quotation may suggest. The reader who wants to study these prophets further might try some of these works, though there are two smaller volumes which I might mention here: William Holladay's *Jeremiah: Spokesman out of Time* (United Church Press, Philadelphia, 1974); and H. Wheeler Robinson's *The Cross in the Old Testament* (out of print). The best full commentaries on the books, in my view, are Claus Westermann's *Isaiah 40-66* (SCM/Westminster Press, 1969) and J.A. Thompson's *Jeremiah* (Eerdmans, 1980).

For quotations from the Bible, I have sometimes used the standard translations, the RSV (Revised Standard Version), JB (Jerusalem Bible), NEB (New English Bible), and GNB (Good

News Bible: Today's English Version); I am glad to acknowledge the use of these. Often they vary from each other, however (and commentaries on the books extend the range of possible interpretations of passages). I have had to come to my own conclusions at such points, and in the pages that follow I have therefore usually provided my own translation though I have not neglected to adopt happy renderings of particular phrases from the standard translations!

Introduction

The Bible begins with an epic story of some quarter of a million words. It opens in Genesis with the creating of order, meaning, and life out of formlessness, emptiness, and nothingness. It closes in 2 Kings with order, meaning, and life disappearing into formlessness, emptiness, and nothingness. The independent existence of the Israelite nation in Palestine collapses with an air of finality as her land is invaded and despoiled, her cities and central shrine are devastated, and her leadership is transported in chains to Babylon.

The affliction of the Israelite people in this period of defeat and exile is mirrored in the story of the prophet Jeremiah (who went through the years leading up to exile with his people) and in the portrayal of the enigmatic servant figure(s) of whom we read in Isaiah 40-55. The affliction of Israel and the affliction of the prophet or the servant are not identical in significance, however. The suffering of the nation as a whole is seen (in these prophetic books and elsewhere) as the deserved punishment of the unfaithfulness to God and injustice among men which characterized Israel. But the affliction of Jeremiah and the servant is unmerited. Strikingly, the moment of deserved punishment is also the occasion which raises the question of undeserved suffering as sharply as any period of Old Testament history did.

Jeremiah and Isaiah 40-55 tackle this problem as an urgent

challenge to practical theology, not as an exercise in philo-
sophical theology in an abstract sense. They are concerned
with the existential question of finding meaning in affliction.
Why does being a prophet involve the experiences it does?
How does a prophet know that the word which costs him so
much really comes from God? How can he remain faithful to
his calling amidst all the pressures to abandon it? These are
some of Jeremiah's questions. They are taken further in the
servant prophecies of Isaiah 40-55, where there is the most
profound realization in the Old Testament of what must be
involved in being God's servant if that calling is to achieve his
deepest purpose.

The questions taken up by these two books are perennial
ones. The vision of 'the servant church' is one which ever
confronts Christians with a challenge that seems at point after
point way beyond anything we have yet taken seriously. For
the calling of the servant was not intended to be something
special, only for the Jeremiahs or the Jesuses of this world.
This was simply what was involved in being the people of
God. It was, one might say, a very democratic notion.

Nor is the world inclined to be patient of prophets if they
fulfil their calling and say the straightest things even to those
in the highest power. The killing of the Archbishop of
Uganda, Janani Luwum, in March 1977 was a particularly
striking example. The church, too, is often impatient of
prophets, particularly when she is on the verge or in the midst
of the exile experience—enfeebled, discredited, defeated,
demoralized. So even those whose only purpose is to get the
church to face the truth ought not to be surprised if they are
made to feel rather like Jeremiah.

His self-portrait thus issues its challenges to Christian
believers in general, though in particular to two archetypal
kinds of believer. The first is the person who is triumphant in
his Christian living and his Christian service, the one to
whom the Lord always seem to be real, who is always full of
the Lord's praise, who seems to be followed by blessing wher-
ever he goes: the Christian who is triumphant, and in danger
of being triumphalist. Jeremiah reminds us, as does Paul,
centuries later, that triumph and affliction usually go
together in the faith of the Bible. Triumph, blessing, and

praise are most authentic when there is a cross at the heart of them. Jeremiah is a man who before Christ embodies a saying of Christ: 'If a man would come after me, *let him deny himself and take up his cross* and follow me' (Mark 8:34). The glory of God and the triumph of God tend to be tied up with crosses. There is a contrast here with the glib promises that sometimes characterize the preaching of the gospel, the easy offers of freedom, harmony, and joy available in Christ to the bound, the broken, and the joyless. Christ brings also a cross, and a cross itself means disharmony. It means not peace, but a sword. That is how it was for Jeremiah.

But Jeremiah's story illustrates a converse truth also, and here it speaks to the opposite kind of person: the one who finds that the parts of the Bible he can easily identify with and find himself in are the parts which talk about doubt, affliction, and protest, which speak of the difficulty of believing and of the implausibility of the faith. Over the past decade, for instance, there has been an increased interest in scholarly circles in the wisdom books of the Old Testament, and part of the reason for this is the fact that there, in Job and Ecclesiastes, it is men's doubts and protests that are the authors' point of departure. Bishop Stuart Blanch *begins* his book on the Old Testament, *For All Mankind*, with Ecclesiastes. In Paul, similarly, many of us find ourselves able to identify with the experience of 2 Corinthians at least as readily as with that of Romans or 1 Corinthians. Among the prophets it is Jeremiah, or his spiritual grandfather Hosea, who represents this message. He is quite open about his protests, his questions, his affliction, and his doubts. He admits when he is defea*ted*, though he is not in the end defea*tist*.

Here, in fact, is the lesson on which he offers so much insight: how to be triumphant without being triumphalist, and how to be defeated without being defeatist. He shows us, in fact, that the key lies in relating these two experiences, triumph and defeat, to each other. We have *treasure*, but in *earthen vessels* ...

Always carrying in the body the death of Jesus, so that the life of Jesus may also be manifested in our bodies.... We are always being given up to death for Jesus' sake, so that

*the life of Jesus may be manifested in our mortal flesh (2
Cor. 4:7,10,11, RSV).*

The prophet and the servant suggest to us what it means to
have treasure in earthen vessels.

But before we go on to look at the books of Jeremiah and
Isaiah, some comments need to be made concerning the
origin of the material we shall be considering. If you look
through a few pages of the book of Jeremiah, you will see
that much of the material is not Jeremiah's poems or sermons
but stories about Jeremiah, or about events in his time (see,
for instance, chapters 37-44). These stories about Jeremiah
were apparently collected after the fall of Jerusalem by Jews
who now saw that he had been right, and that it was therefore important to understand what he has been doing. For the
same reason, they collected his teaching so that they and their
contemporaries could take it more seriously than it had been
taken before the exile. Now these men were not merely concerned to preserve the message of Jeremiah out of an anti-
quarian interest in the past. They wanted to bring a message
to the present, to the time of exile in which they themselves
lived. They wanted to apply Jeremiah's teaching to their own
day, because they believed it was God's word and had a
message for them.
    But this introduces a complication for us. How far are they
relating to us exactly what Jeremiah said; how far are they
applying his message to their own age? Broadly speaking,
scholars agree that the passages printed as poetry in modern
Bibles go back to Jeremiah himself. The passages printed in
ordinary prose, however, may well be later sermons preached on texts from Jeremiah's words, or may be what these
preachers in the exile believed ought to be said in their day by
Jews who wanted to continue Jeremiah's ministry. Some of
what we have in the book of Jeremiah, then, is not what Jeremiah actually was and said in his own day, but what he
meant to people who lived in the exile and who now wanted
to help people to see that he had spoken the word of the Lord
and must still be listened to.
    If this is right, then the book of Jeremiah is not a contem-

porary photograph of the prophet, but a later portrait of
him; or rather, contemporary records (the poetry) are set in
the context of later perspective (the prose). And overall, we
are enriched. In the chapters that follow, I shall not be trying
to isolate the contemporary record from the later perspective, but reading the material as it stands as the account
of what Jeremiah meant to those who looked back on his
ministry.

When we move on to consider the motif of the servant in
Isaiah 40-55, a parallel (though different) issue arises. Here is
the message of the book of Isaiah to the Jewish people in exile
in the sixth century BC. But the prophet Isaiah lived in the
eighth century BC. How did there come to be so many chapters of prophecies to the people in exile in a book that comes
from two hundred years previously? There are two main possible answers. One is that, despite the difference in date, all
sixty-six chapters in the book came from the prophet Isaiah
whose name appears at the beginning of it. On this view,
since God *could* have revealed this message to Isaiah, there is
no reason not to take the book at its face value; we may
assume that he *did* reveal to Isaiah the message destined for
those who would be in exile much later. The other approach
is to assume that the book as a whole is more of an anthology
than this first view implies. The work began as the ministry
of Isaiah, but later messages were added to his by prophets
who brought God's word to subsequent periods. There are
links between the different parts of the book (for instance, a
favourite title for God throughout is the phrase 'the holy one
of Israel'), and these may suggest that the authors of the later
prophecies believed that God had given them the mantle that
Isaiah once wore, just as Elisha had literally worn the mantle
of Elijah (2 Kings 1).

I myself think that, while God *could* indeed have revealed
the messages in Isaiah 40-55 two centuries before the exile, it
is difficult to see why he *would* have done so. They were
irrelevant to the eighth century. So I assume that they are the
words of a prophet who lived in Babylon in the exile, and I
shall refer to him as 'the prophet', or as 'Isaiah of the exile'
(because he did seem to view himself as bringing to his day
the message that Isaiah would have brought had he still been

alive).

It may be that the reader finds it difficult to accept these approaches to the origin of the material in Jeremiah and Isaiah 40-55. If so, it may be worth noting that it makes little difference to the meaning of the books: Cyrus the Persian is Cyrus the Persian living in the time of the exile, whenever the book was written!

Jeremiah
'It is like a burning fire in my heart'
(Jeremiah 20.9)

CHAPTER ONE

What being a prophet costs

So Jeremiah is the 2 Corinthians of the Old Testament. Now I have read somewhere that in the New Testament there is a suggestive sequence in the way Romans, 1 Corinthians, and 2 Corinthians follow each other. When the gospel of grace is boldly preached, as it is in Romans, it will cause a revolution whose spin-off may be the troubles reflected in 1 Corinthians. Then, dealing with these traumas may well cost the preacher himself, as 2 Corinthians shows it cost Paul.

In the Old Testament, Isaiah 1-39 might be seen as an equivalent to Romans. Here the election love of God is clearly declared: despite the sin of Judah God will keep his promise to David; he will not let Jerusalem fall. This promise of God's grace is only too enthusiastically received, and Israel gains new confidence in God's irrevocable commitment to her. But she becomes deaf to that note in her faith which spoke of the demands God makes on those to whom he commits himself. Thus there run through subsequent prophets, including Jeremiah, indictment after indictment of the wantonness of Israel: of her moral laxity, her broken relationships, her social disorder, her faithless worship, her twisted theology. The charges are quite parallel to those of 1 Corinthians. But interwoven with these indictments in Jeremiah is the other note to

15

which we have drawn attention, the record of the struggles and affliction of the prophet himself. Dealing with the troubles of Judah brought its personal cost to Jeremiah. Here is the Paul of 2 Corinthians, as it were.

Jeremiah unveils his own experience of being continually given up to death, his own proving of what being a prophet costs, in a series of prayers and protests which are grouped together in chapters 11-20 of his book. These poems are often referred to as the 'confessions' of Jeremiah, but this is a misleading description. They are not passages in which Jeremiah is confessing his sin, or even, generally, confessing the greatness of God. They are the lamentations of Jeremiah. As far as their form goes, they are like the laments in the psalter, in which believers pour out their suffering, their anger, and their longings to God.

They come quite early in Jeremiah's book, and it has often been inferred that they thus belong to a relatively early stage in his ministry; that they record the spiritual crisis he experienced at that point as he wrestled with the cost of being a prophet. It was, on this view, a crisis he came through triumphantly, so that when we see Jeremiah confronting Jehoiakim or Hananiah or Zekediah later on in the book, when we see him hauled before the temple authorities and put in the stocks (as we do in chapter 20), or threatened with the death sentence (chapter 26), or imprisoned in the court of the guard (chapter 32), or dying of hunger in a disused water cistern (chapter 38), or bound in chains by the Babylonians (chapter 40) or ridiculed by Hananiah (chapter 28) or ignored by Jehoiakim (chapter 36) or contradicted by Azariah (chapter 43)—when we see him *outwardly* afflicted, we see nevertheless a man who had already walked through the fires and come out the other side, who now through it all stands confident, firm, unwavering and resolute. Inner doubt is resolved and strength of faith is now triumphant.

In subsequent chapters, Jeremiah is indeed outwardly unwavering and resolute. But I wonder if we are to assume that he had long ago won the final victory over his inner turmoil, and was never any more tempted to give up in despair. The mere fact that the laments are collected at this point in the book does not entitle us to make the assumption that inner turmoil belonged to only one chronological period. Admittedly chapters 11-20 major on his inner suffering while chapters 26-45 concentrate on his outward affliction. But the book of Jeremiah is not arranged chronologically, and I suspect that these are two aspects of his continuing prophetic calling. This double experience, of inner suffering and outward affliction, characterized his ministry all through.

Perhaps the very fact that the last of the confessions (last, that is, in the arrangement of the book), in chapter 20, closes with despair and not confidence warns against our understanding these passages as reflecting an admittedly deep but essentially passing spiritual turmoil. And what was true of the inward affliction, that it ends on a down note, ends in turmoil, is true also of the outward suffering. Of course, Jeremiah does have his good moments. In a paradoxical way the fall of Jerusalem is one, because that is the point at which he is proved right, when it is established that God has not been fooling him. But even then his message is not taken to heart, and the man who had been dragged by his heels into Jerusalem at the beginning of his ministry (chapter 1) is now dragged by his heels out of Jerusalem at the end of his ministry, taken as a lucky charm by Jews who have decided that the only future lies in refuge in Egypt (chapter 43). As Gerhard von Rad points out in his *Old Testament Theology* (Volume 2, 1966, p.207), no ravens feed Jeremiah as they fed Elijah. No angel stops the lions' mouth for him, as one did for Daniel. So almost our last sight of Jeremiah is his back as he turns his feet wearily south, his ministry apparently fruitless, his future apparently only death, far away from the inheritance that he had promised that he and his brethren would repossess in Palestine (chapters 32-33). The story of his outward suffering, like that of his inward affliction, ends in misery. In various ways, then, Jeremiah had to pay the cost of being a prophet.

TO STAND ALONE

One element in that cost is that Jeremiah has to be willing to stand alone, to cope with isolation, opposition, betrayal, and attack, even from those who ought to be most loyal to him.

Chapter 11 begins with the notes of a sermon by Jeremiah in which he calls on Judah to take seriously the covenant (the solemnly agreed mutual commitment) between herself and Yahweh. But as the sermon notes develop they make it clear that, as far as Jeremiah can see, there is no prospect of that challenge being met. This generation, like previous generations, is totally unresponsive to God, beyond praying for, and destined for judgement.

> The word which came to Jeremiah from Yahweh. 'Speak to the men who live in Judah and Jerusalem. Say to them, Yahweh, the God of Israel says: "A curse rests on everyone who does not obey these terms of the covenant which I issued to your ancestors at the time when I brought them out of Egypt, out of the smelting furnace." I said, "Listen to my voice and act in accordance with everything that I tell you. You will be my people and I myself will be your God. This will lead to my keeping the oath which I swore to your ancestors, that I would give them a land where milk and honey flow"—as they now have.' I answered, 'I will, Lord' (11:1-5).

The chapter begins uncontroversially enough; it is very reminiscent of the warnings of Deuteronomy 27. But it goes on,

> Then Yahweh said to me, 'Proclaim all these things in the cities of Judah and the streets of Jerusalem: Listen to these terms of the covenant and act on them, because I solemnly charged your ancestors at the time when I brought them up from Egypt, and I have continued to do so until today. I have gone out of my way to charge them to listen to my voice. But they did not listen. They did not give me their attention; to a man they lived in accordance with their stubborn, evil inclinations. So I brought on them all the sanctions of the covenant; I had issued it for them to act on, and they had not' (11:6-8).

The polemic is beginning. The demand of obedience, Jeremiah declares, was never met. The nation to a man behaved in a way contrary to Yahweh's will. This claim about the past presages what is to follow about the present generation:

> Then Yahweh said to me, 'A conspiracy has emerged
> among the men who live in Judah and Jerusalem. They
> have gone back to the perverse ways of their earliest ances-
> tors, who refused to listen to my words. They have fol-
> lowed the worship of other gods. Israel and Judah have
> broken the covenant I made with their ancestors. This is
> what Yahweh therefore says: "I am now going to bring
> upon them a disaster which they will not be able to evade.
> They can cry out to me but I will not listen to them. The
> cities of Judah and the inhabitants of Jerusalem can go and
> cry to the gods to whom they offer up sacrifices, though
> they will certainly not save them in the hour of disaster.
> You, Judah, have a god for every city, and in every street
> of Jerusalem you have put an altar for shame itself, an altar
> for offering up sacrifices to Baal" (11:9-13).

Resistance characterizes the present generation as much as it
has previous ones. It runs so deep it cannot be undone, nor its
punishment averted.

> 'So you yourself may not pray for this people. Raise no
> cries or prayers for her. I shall not be listening when they
> call on me in their hour of disaster. What place has my
> beloved in my house, with her devices? Can vows and con-
> secrated meat remove the evil from her? Then you could
> be jubilant! "A beautiful, verdant olive-tree with lovely
> fruit", Yahweh described you. With a roar like thunder he
> will set fire to it, and its branches will break. The Almighty
> Yahweh who planted you has threatened you with disaster
> because of the wrong which Israel and Judah themselves
> have done. They have made me angry by burning offerings
> to Baal' (11:14-17).

It is difficult to imagine a more swingeing or unequivocal
condemnation of his people than Jeremiah delivers here. Now
for Jeremiah to speak like this in the temple could only place
him in great danger; we may again recall the death of Archbishop Luwum after writing a quite diplomatically-phrased
letter. Jeremiah's sermon constituted a threatening challenge
to both church and state (Israel's glory and her perennial

problem was that both were the same). All the vested interests would instinctively combine to crush his message. That
was quite obvious; though to Jeremiah, obvious only with
hindsight.

> *It was Yahweh who made it known to me, thus I knew. At
> that time you opened my eyes to what they had done. But I
> was like a pet lamb being taken to the butcher's—I did not
> know that they were hatching plots against me (11:18-19).*

'They' are the men of Anathoth (11:21), Jeremiah's home
village, an hour's walk from Jerusalem. Jeremiah perhaps
naively hoped that his message would be listened to, that at
least his own villagers might be expected to be on his side. But
their own countries tend to be the last places that show
honour to prophets.

> *Let's destroy the tree as well as its fruit (11:19).*

Let's make sure, in other words, that it produces nothing else
like this that we've been hearing.

> *Let's cut him off from the land of the living ...*

We have some vivid verbs in English to make the point: he
must be eliminated, exterminated, annihilated.

> *... so that his name will not be remembered any more.*

Old Testament believers were granted only a rather vague
understanding of life after death (perhaps because the resurrection of the dead would be possible only when Christ had
died and been raised as the firstfruits of that general resurrection) and thus they valued other assurances that physical
death was not the complete end of them. One of these was the
realization that their name lived on in the name and in the
memory of their descendants. But Jeremiah's attackers want
to deprive him even of that.

God's response to all this is twofold. One element in it is to
declare that the men of Anathoth will not get away with it.

God, too, can use those verbs: Jeremiah's attackers will be eliminated (11:22-23). Jeremiah's prayer for vengeance (11:20) will be answered. But not yet: for the other element in God's response to Jeremiah is less comforting. Jeremiah will have to put up with men like these opponents throughout his ministry. 'You'll just have to get a grip, Jeremiah, because things are going to get worse before they get better'.

> *If you raced with men on foot, and they have wearied you,*
> *how will you get on against horses? (12:5).*

'Jeremiah, have you heard of handicap races? Well, you are entered for one. You are running, they are in chariots. Ready, steady, go!' Or, to put it another way, 'Jeremiah, you cannot afford to relax even in what looks like easy country. Even in a land of peace where things ought to be safe, you've got to learn to be on your guard; because you have to go through territory that's more like the wild undergrowth along the Jordan, where a snake may be curled under a leaf or a lion be lurking behind the next tree. You've got to learn to be on your guard' (cf. 12:5b). There are no lions in Palestine now. But in those days, down by the Jordan you had to be on your guard. And Jeremiah has to learn to live that way even in territory that *looks* safe.

> *Because even your brothers and your father's house,*
> *even they have betrayed you.*
> *Even they are in full cry behind you.*
> *Do not believe them,*
> *even though they speak nice words to you (12:6).*

A prophet has no honour in his own country *and among his own kin and in his own house* (Mark 6:4). In fact, a prophet has to be willing to stand alone.

TO HAVE NO PRIVATE LIFE

Another element in the cost of being a prophet, for Jeremiah, was to have no private life. He had no freedom to make his own decisions about how he lived his life; indeed he was forbidden the life of a normal human being. He had already lost the family in which he was brought up: *Your brothers and your father's house ... are in full cry behind you* (12:6). He is allowed no other family to replace that: *You are not to take a wife, nor are you to have sons or daughters in this place* (16:2).

Now normally even the person who has no family has his place in the wider community. When occasions of grief or celebration come, he joins in them. But this, too, is forbidden to Jeremiah. No rejoicing with those who rejoice, no weeping with those who weep (16:5,8). Jeremiah had to be a man apart. He was denied these normal human experiences.

It was not because Jeremiah was 'gay' that he did not marry, nor was it because he was a loner that he cut himself off from fasting and feasting. It was because this was part of God's calling. His very life was to be part of his preaching. In a sense, of course, it always is. But in a special sense with Jeremiah at this point. 'Jeremiah, *why* don't you get married?' (It was a very unusual decision for a man to take in Israel; indeed the married majority still suspect the unmarried minority). 'Because Jerusalem at this point of time is no place to be setting up family, no place to be bringing up children'.

For this is Yahweh's message concerning the sons and daughters born in this place, the mothers who bear them and the fathers who beget them in this land. They will die of terrible afflictions, and not be lamented or buried. They will be manure spread on the ground. They will meet their end by sword and by famine, and their corpses will be food for the birds of the air and the animals on the ground (16:3-4).

So the prophet's action was part of his message.

Again, 'Why doesn't Jeremiah join with those who mourn —has he no feelings?' 'Because the suffering that is to be experienced here in Jerusalem is so terrible that there will be no comfort; indeed there will be no-one left to mourn.'

High and low in this land will die. They will not be buried,

*or lamented. No-one will gash himself or shave his head
for them. No-one will break mourning bread to comfort
someone bereaved, or give them the cup of comfort for
their father and mother (16:6-7).*

'I am having no sorrowing here, I am withdrawing all consolation, I am refusing all comfort, because of the state of this
people'.

'And why doesn't Jeremiah join in the celebration of
weddings and anniversaries and birthdays?' Because the im-
pending doom of Jerusalem makes celebration grotesque.

*For this is the message of Almighty Yahweh, the God of
Israel. 'Now, before your own eyes and in your own times
I am putting an end to the sound of joy and gladness, the
voice of groom and bride, in this place' (16:9).*

Jeremiah's personal life helps to make the point. He cannot
take a man's normal place in his people's life, since God's purpose requires something different. He can show no natural
feelings; if he wishes to sorrow with someone he cannot; he
cannot marry. He is God's servant, and being a servant
means having no feelings of his own or desires of his own. It
means being completely at God's disposal in the totality of his
private life. Jeremiah reminds us of Hosea, who was told to
marry a woman who would turn out to be an adulteress, or
of Ezekiel, who was told not to mourn his wife when she
died. Alongside these we may set the prohibition on Jeremiah
marrying at all. The demand of God for a devotion which
expresses itself in total obedience may mean one has no private life. In a sense one has no basic human rights at all.

TO BE AS HARD AS A ROCK OUTSIDE EVEN WHILE YOU ARE
BEING TORN APART INSIDE

*Jeremiah took his stand in the court of Yahweh's house and
said to all the people:
These are the words of Almighty Yahweh, the God of
Israel: 'I am going to bring on this city and upon all its*

*cities all the trouble that I have spoken of, because they
have resolutely refused to listen to my words.'
Pashhur the priest, the son of Immer, who was in supreme
authority in Yahweh's house, heard Jeremiah prophesying
these things. Pashhur had Jeremiah the prophet flogged
and put in the stocks at the upper Benjamin Gate of
Yahweh's house. Next day Pashhur released Jeremiah from
the stocks; Jeremiah then said to him:
'Pashhur is not the name Yahweh has given you, but rather
Magor-missabib, Terror-on-all-sides. For these are Yahweh's words: "I am going to make you a terror to yourself
and to all your friends. They will fall by the sword of their
enemies before your very eyes. I shall give the whole of
Judah into the power of the king of Babylon. He will take
some into exile in Babylon and put others to the sword. I
shall hand over to their enemies all this city's resources, all
its gains, all its treasures, all the wealth of the kings of
Judah. They will seize them as loot and take them to
Babylon. And you yourself, Pashhur, you and all your
household, will go into captivity. To Babylon you shall
go, there you will die, and there you will be buried, you
and all your friends to whom you have prophesied lies"'
(19:14b-20:6).*

Despite the treatment he receives from the temple authorities,
Jeremiah here appears as a man who can be hard as a rock
when he is under huge pressure to change his stance and modify his message. Jeremiah is quite resolute. Yet immediately
afterwards (in the arrangement of the material in the book of
Jeremiah) we find the forthright prophet suddenly on his
knees in despair. It was despite himself that he became a prophet, and (in the light of experiences such as this one) it is
despite himself that he remains one. He protests not merely
about human opposition but about the divine force that is
used against him.

*You used your persuasion, Yahweh, and I was persuaded;
you were too strong for me and you overcame me.
I am an object of derision all the time,
all of them laugh at me,
because whenever I speak, I cry for help:
'Violence', 'outrage', I declare,*

> *because Yahweh's word has come to mean*
> *scorn and ridicule for me all the time (20:7-8).*

Jeremiah was called to be a prophet in 626 B.C., and from that
point began to declare the message of judgement expressed
above in his words to Pashhur. But decades pass and the
judgement never arrives. The city remains in one piece. Jeremiah is still prophesying, but he has lost credibility; he has
become a figure of fun. Underneath the mocking there may
still be some fear, lest Jeremiah should turn out to be right
after all (perhaps Pashhur's attempt to silence him implies as
much). But he is nevertheless a public laughing stock. He has
to declare a message that never seems to come true. *They say
to me, 'Where is Yahweh's word? Let it come true, if it can!'*
(17:15). 'Come on, Jeremiah, all these gloomy words about
the collapse of the state, about the judgement of God upon
the nation. Come on, let's see it happen then. Fine words of
yours, Jeremiah, but they don't come true. Where is Yahweh's word? Let it come true, if it can!' Being a servant of
God here involves being apparently abandoned and made a
fool of *both* by men *and* by God.

So what should Jeremiah do? Obviously, he should pack
up his scroll and go home. But that is just what he cannot do.

> *If I say I will put him out of my mind,*
> *I will not speak in his name any more,*
> *then it is like a burning fire in my heart,*
> *imprisoned within my body.*
> *I weary myself holding on to it,*
> *and I cannot do so (20:9).*

The fire of the wrath of God burns inside him and has to find
expression. God not only browbeat him into becoming a prophet in the first place (20:7); he allows him no escape now.
He has him and will not let him go. 'The cosmic sadist, who
plays with me as his pawn, requires me to warn people about
a calamity which isn't going to happen, and gives me no
choice but to co-operate. Catch 22'.

'I have no choice' is clearly very negative. But in another
sense it may have a positive implication. Jeremiah has, at

least in theory, decided to try turning his back on God and on
his calling. But he has found that he cannot. He is a man in a
dark room who has found the door, and discovered that it is
locked on the other side. So at least he knows where he is,
and the purpose of it all may seem mysterious, but the possibility that there *is* a meaningful purpose is not decreased by
his discovery. Indeed, it is increased.

Von Rad summarizes Jeremiah's position in these words:

> The picture we see is of a man appointed to hear the word
> of God. As a result of this divine call he surrenders much
> of his freedom—occasionally he is completely overwhelmed
> by an external compulsion: but paradoxically, just because
> he has received this call he is able to enjoy an entirely new
> kind of freedom. Drawn into ever more and more close
> converse with God, he is privy to the divine purposes and
> is thereby given the authority to enter into a unique kind
> of converse with men. The man reflected here is not, of
> course, an integrated personality. He is divided and sorely
> troubled as God hides himself from him more and more.
> Yet, as the martyrdom of Jeremiah testifies, he is in some
> mysterious way free to choose suffering and so to stand up
> to God's test (*Old Testament Theology*, Volume 2, p.76).

In an article on 'The theological significance of doubt in the
Old Testament' (*Annual of the Swedish Theological Institute*
7, 1968-9, p.47), Robert Davidson put Jeremiah's position
more briefly in the question, 'If he had never said "I'll forget
him" would he ever have affirmed so positively "I can't"?'

So Jeremiah, though outwardly resolute, is inwardly torn
apart by humiliation. He is also torn apart by fear. Here we
return to the note which appeared in chapter 11.

> *I have heard many people whispering:*
> *'There is terror on all sides!*
> *Report him, let's report him!'*
> *All my friends are watching for my downfall.*
> *'Perhaps he can be persuaded and prevailed over,*
> *then we can catch him and take vengeance on him' (20:10).*

Jeremiah is terrified of the danger he is in at the hand of those who have turned against him. The pressure is real, though it makes one ask whether he has forgotten about Yahweh, forgotten indeed the words he himself wrote a few pages ago:

> *Happy the man who trusts in Yahweh,*
> *whose trust is Yahweh.*
> *He is like a tree planted by water,*
> *sending out its roots by a stream.*
> *It is not afraid when hot weather comes,*
> *its leaves stay green.*
> *In a year of drought it is not anxious,*
> *it does not stop producing fruit (17:7-8).*

Jeremiah has not, in fact, forgotten those declarations of faith. The kind of prayer that Jeremiah has been praying appears also in the psalms, and there it characteristically leads to an expression of confidence in and praise to the God who does answer prayer. The psalmists get things off their chests to God and thus pass their burdens on to him; they can then praise him for taking the burden from them, for hearing prayer and promising to answer it. That is how the life of prayer is supposed to work. Jeremiah, too, makes this transition from urgent prayer or protest (20:7-10) to a declaration of trust in God (20:11), followed by a specific petition for matters to be put right (20:12), and then by confession of his praise (20:13). Having expressed his inner turmoil, he thus goes on to declare that he has confidence in Yahweh, nevertheless.

> *But Yahweh is with me like a fearsome warrior.*
> *Therefore my persecutors will stumble, they will not prevail.*
> *They will be bitterly ashamed because they have not succeeded.*
> *Their disgrace will last for ever, it will not be forgotten.*
> *Almighty Yahweh, righteous in his testing,*
> *the one who sees into heart and mind,*
> *let me see your vengeance upon them,*
> *since it was to you that I committed my cause.*
> *Sing to Yahweh, praise Yahweh!*
> *He rescues the needy from the power of evil men!*
> $\qquad\qquad\qquad\qquad\qquad$ *(20:11-13).*

But these words of confidence, expectation, and praise are not the end of what Jeremiah has to say to God. He cannot, in fact, quite hold on to this conviction that God is with him. He has not forgotten those words about trust. But he is torn apart because faith and praise wrestle for possession of his heart with doubt and despair, and he cannot quite endure the strain of this tension.

> *Curse the day I was born!*
> *May the day my mother bore me never be blessed!*
> *Curse the man who brought the news to my father,*
> *'It's a boy! You have had a son!',*
> *making him so glad.*
> *May that man be like the cities*
> *that Yahweh overthrew without pity,*
> *may he hear a cry in the morning*
> *and an alarm at noon,*
> *because he did not kill me at birth,*
> *so that my mother would have become my grave,*
> *and her womb would have been enlarged for ever.*
> *Why did I come out of the womb,*
> *to see trouble and affliction*
> *and end my life in disgrace?* (20:14-18).

Sing to Yahweh, praise Yahweh (verse 13); *curse the day I was born* (verse 14). Who is this man who proclaims that God is judge, *and* that God commits violence and outrage; who declares God's praise, *and* curses the day he was born; who is as hard as a rock outside, but torn apart inside?

The most extraordinary thing is that the chapter ends on that note of despair. Sharing your experiences with other people is relatively easy, when it means acknowledging that you *have been* going through a bad patch, but that the Lord has now brought you out of it. Here is a man who puts into writing where he is spiritually even though that means ending in total blackness. He had no choice and he found no release, because God needed someone to keep warning Judah about the calamity that was coming, and he had to keep living by faith (and not by sight) over the question of whether God was ever going to fulfil his word.

But why did he write it down? It is rather surprising to find this anti-testimony in a prophetic book. There is nothing quite like it elsewhere in the prophets, though Jeremiah's final cry of despair is paralleled and developed in Job. The other prophets do not tell us much of the intimacy of their relationship with God. Why does Jeremiah do so? Why is there recorded in Scripture the personal and private agonizing of the man of God with God?

One reason may arise out of the fact that it is obviously not easy to be hard as a rock outside when you are being torn apart inside. The tension between the outward proclamation and the inner scream itself threatens to rend the man apart. The scream, indeed, cannot finally be stifled or repressed. It has to receive expression. So writing it down helps to give expression to it in the only way that is possible. It gets it out of the system. That may be one reason why Jeremiah put it in writing.

That is itself striking. But even more remarkable is the fact that Jeremiah's agonizing finds a place in God's book. God, in other words, accepted Jeremiah's complaints and protests and prayers for vengeance on his enemies. God let Jeremiah batter him on the chest, and encourages us to follow Jeremiah's example. We too may be called to stand hard as a rock. But if, as we have to do so outwardly, we are torn apart inwardly, that inward affliction can receive expression. We need not attempt to bottle it up, because God invites us to pour it out. We do not have to deny it; we can acknowledge it to ourselves and to God. We can be honest to God.

Now there is such a thing as effrontery or cheek, such a thing as failure to treat God as God. The point at which boldness becomes effrontery depends in part on the pressure a man has been put under, on the demands that have been laid upon him. Jeremiah is a man on whom God made total demands. He is a man who comes close to a total commitment. And the man of a unique obedience is entitled to a unique boldness.

I remember once noticing a poster on Nottingham Railway Station: 'There is a religion which sees life as a challenge to be met, not as a cross to be born.' If there is, then it is not the religion of Jeremiah, nor of Jesus. Nor is it a religion I am very interested in. Because a religion that is worth following has to be able to cope with the fact that life is not always a thrilling challenge; it is sometimes an experience of crucifixion. And being a prophet, or being any kind of faithful servant of God, is not always a thrilling challenge. Sometimes, the experience of the cost of isolation and opposition, of the loss of any right to run one's own life, of being torn apart even as one is as hard as a rock outside, is rather an experience of crucifixion.

Indeed, arguably, it is at these moments of crucifixion that Christian ministry is at its most authentic, its most distinctive. For that was how it was with Jesus, and that is how it is with the person who follows Jesus.

The parallels between Jeremiah and Jesus are striking. Both experienced isolation and betrayal by those nearest to them; the loss of family and home and a permanent place to lay one's head; being inwardly torn apart (in Gethsemane, in Jesus' case) even while they were hard as a rock outside (in the temple or on trial). It is hardly surprising that some people, when asked who they thought Jesus was, suggested he might be Jeremiah reincarnate. Jesus supremely fulfils Jeremiah's kind of calling.

But this does not imply that henceforth God's servants never have to do so. On the contrary, the cost of following Christ is to take up your own cross. When Paul was converted, the Lord described him as 'a chosen instrument of mine. For I will show him how much he must suffer for the sake of my name' (Acts 9:15-16).

> ... always being given up to death for Jesus' sake, so that the life of Jesus may be manifested in our mortal flesh (2 Cor. 4:11).

That is how *Christian* ministry works.

There is a cost involved in being a prophet, in being a servant of God. There is a cross involved. We do not have to hide from this fact with glib talk about life being a challenge. Because God promises that as we carry the cross, we can also reveal the glory. Even unknowingly, in his blackest moments, Jeremiah was doing that; how, will emerge more clearly as we consider who a prophet is identified with.

CHAPTER TWO

Who a prophet is identified with

Why is such a cost involved in being a prophet? How is God's glory revealed in his affliction? In his book on *The Prophets*, the American rabbi Abraham Heschel talks about Jeremiah's sympathy: his sympathy with Israel, and his sympathy with God. Jeremiah feels with, shares the emotions of, Yahweh's people, and Yahweh himself. He is identified with them. It is this identification which costs Jeremiah.

IDENTIFICATION WITH ISRAEL

Jeremiah was a prophet of doom. He was a man who talked about terror on all sides, and who declared that the collapse of the state was inevitable. How is one to visualize his face as he delivers this message? Would it have an air of triumph and satisfaction? Is Jeremiah the kind of preacher of doom whose message really gives expression to his own hang-ups?

One must grant that Jeremiah had no quarrel with God over whether Jerusalem should be destroyed, and in this sense he would be triumphant and satisfied when it was. But at the same time he was identified with Israel in her affliction. He accepted, but dreaded, her destruction. He prayed for it to be averted. And he accepted a share in her calling and in her suffering.

His anguish finds clear expression in his moving poem concerning a drought which apparently occurred one year in Judah.

> *Judah droops, her cities languish,*
> *her men sink to the ground;*
> *Jerusalem's cry goes up.*
> *Their flock-masters send their boys for water;*
> *they come to the pools but find no water there.*
> *Back they go, with empty vessels,*
> *the produce of the land has failed,*
> *because there is no rain.*
> *The farmers' hopes are wrecked,*
> *they uncover their heads for grief.*
> *The hind calves in the open country and forsakes her young*
>   *because there is no grass;*
> *for lack of herbage, wild asses stand on the high bare places*
>   *and snuff the wind for moisture,*
> *as wolves do, and their eyes begin to fail (14:2-6 NEB).*

So Jeremiah speaks concerning a present calamity. But a prophet is a man of insight, of foresight, of a vivid imagination. He experiences also things that still belong to the future. Jeremiah goes through all the horror and panic of enemy invasion, before it actually occurs.

> *I am in anguish! I writhe with pain!*
> *Walls of my heart!*
> *My heart is throbbing!*
> *I cannot keep quiet,*
> *for I have heard the trumpet call*
> *and the cry of war.*
> *Ruin on ruin is the news:*
> *the whole land is laid waste ...*

It is as if there has been a nuclear holocaust that leaves nothing on earth but the awful stillness of death.

> *I looked to the earth, to see a formless waste;*
> *to the heavens, and their light had gone.*
> *I looked to the mountains, to see them quaking*
> *and all the heights astir.*
> *I looked, to see no man at all,*
> *the very birds of heaven had fled.*
> *I looked, to see the wooded country a wilderness,*
> *all its towns in ruins,*
> *at the presence of Yahweh,*
> *at the presence of his burning anger (4:19-20, 23-26 JB).*

At the presence of Yahweh! It is God who brings about the calamities of the present and of the imminent future. For they are caused by Judah's turning from God and his ways. And so Jeremiah's anguish finds expression in his sadness at her spiritual blindness and her false trust.

> *How can I bear my sorrow? I am sick at heart.*
> *Hark, the cry of my people from a distant land:*
> *'Is the LORD not in Zion? Is her King no longer there?'*
> *Why do they provoke me with their images and foreign*
> *gods?*
> *Harvest is past, summer is over, and we are not saved.*
> *I am wounded at the sight of my people's wound;*
> *I go like a mourner, overcome with horror.*
> *Is there no balm in Gilead, no physician there?*
> *Why has no new skin grown over their wound?*
> *Would that my head were all water, my eyes a fountain*
> *of tears, that I might weep day and night for my*
> *people's dead! (8:18-9:1 NEB).*

There is a twofold blindness here. First, a facile, blithe trust that everything will be all right because God is on our side. 'Is the kingly presence of Yahweh himself not known in Jerusalem, his own royal city?' Yet those who have said, 'Don't worry, the Lord is with us, he is on our side', have often been mistaken. But then there is secondly an inability to recognize that those who seek help from other gods as well as notionally relying on Yahweh thereby actually forfeit Yahweh's help. No hedging of bets is possible.

So one evidence that a prophet is identified with his people is the anguish which he feels, both at their suffering and at their blindness. There is no cheap preaching of the judgement of God. The authentic declaration of God's judgement on church or nation is delivered with tears in the preacher's eyes.

A second expression of a prophet's identification with his people is the fact that he prays for them. Intercession was an integral part of a prophet's calling. His task was not only to speak on God's behalf to man, but also to speak on man's behalf to God. Indeed, Jeremiah grants that if he had not prayed for his people, they would have had every reason for resentment against him (18:20). But he had prayed for them. The poem concerning the drought, for instance, continues as the prayer in which Jeremiah leads the people on the occasion of this disaster.

> *Though our sins testify against us,*
> *yet act, O LORD, for thy own name's sake ...*
> *Thou art in our midst, O LORD,*
> *and thou hast named us thine; do not forsake us ...*
> *Hast thou spurned Judah utterly?*
> *Dost thou loathe Zion?*
> *Why hast thou wounded us, and there is no remedy;*
> *Why let us hope for better days, and we find nothing good,*
> *for a time of healing, and all is disaster? ...*
> *Can any of the false gods of the nations give rain?*
> *Or do the heavens send showers of themselves?*
> *Art thou not God, O LORD, that we may hope in thee?*
> *It is thou only who doest all these things*
>   *(14:7,9,19,22 NEB).*

Jeremiah prayed, he encouraged them to pray, he prayed on their behalf.

There are actually very few strictly intercessory prayers in the Old Testament. But there are two other kinds of prayers which seem to fulfil a similar function to intercessory prayer, and which may be suggestive for our praying. One is the declaration of God's blessing—'May the people prosper, may the king defend the cause of the poor.' A fair number of psalms declare God's blessing in this way (for instance, Ps. 72), and it is an equivalent to what we might call intercession.

The other kind of prayer is when someone actually identi-fies with someone else in prayer. Praying on their behalf means putting oneself in their place, praying as if one was this other person. If I do that, I pray not for 'them', but for 'us'—I am so identified with them. It is this which is characteristic of Jeremiah's prayers for his people.

We acknowledge our wickedness, the wrongdoing of our fathers. We have sinned against you, Yahweh (14:20).

Jeremiah does not stand aloof from the people in their sin: he identifies with the sinner, as Jesus did in his baptism and on his cross. To intercede for someone involves being identified with them, sharing their situation, standing in their place. Daniel's prayer (Dan. 9) is like this: not *'they* have sinned, please bring them to repentance', but *'we* have sinned, please forgive us'. At first sight, Moses' prayer for the Israelites' for-giveness is rather different: 'This people have committed a gross sin'; but then Moses goes on, 'Please erase my name from your book', if that is the cost of their forgiveness (Exod. 32:31,32). Intercession involves standing in someone else's place out of a willingness to identify with those to whom one has to minister.

We can approach a third aspect to Jeremiah's identification with Israel by asking the question, 'What do we mean by "Israel"?' In an outward sense the answer to that question is clear enough: it is the descendants of the patriarch Israel or Jacob. But in the inward sense, 'Israel' means something rather different. Much later, Paul comments that 'not all who are descended from Israel belong to Israel' (Rom. 9:6). In-deed, in Paul's day *most* of the outward Israel did not belong to the inward Israel. Only a small number, a 'remnant', recognized Jesus as Messiah and showed that they belonged to the real Israel. Paul himself is the epitome of that small minority (see Rom. 11:1-5).

It was the same in Jeremiah's day; the bulk of Israel had turned their backs on being Israel. On that occasion, too, there was one man who epitomized what it meant to be Israel: Jeremiah himself. Before he was even born, he had been chosen by God, formed by God, known by God, conse-

crated by God (1:5). He was called to be the one true
Israelite, called to stand alone, apart from the crowd, to show
the crowd what it should be. His vocation was to incarnate
the response to God which all Israel was supposed to make.
He had to be willing to be a minority of one.

In the modern western world, people do not mind being
distinctive. We enjoy doing our own thing. We would rather
stand out from the crowd than be identified with its grey
mass. But in most cultures people have not wanted to be different. Their identity comes in large part from their identification with a community. Jeremiah did not enjoy having to
be different. But he had to stand alone—and here is a paradox
—precisely because of his identification with Israel. He had to
be identified with the Israel of the flesh, in his anguish and his
prayer. But he also had to be identified with the Israel of the
spirit, to be the minority of one, to be the one true Israelite,
and in this sense to be a man apart.

Of course, it was not God's purpose that responsive Israel
should consist of one man and no more. On the contrary,
Jeremiah's task was to call all Israel to follow. But only a
number in fact respond. One was Baruch, the scribe who
wrote down Jeremiah's prophecies (see Jer. 36). Baruch shared
Jeremiah's response to the Lord, and he shared Jeremiah's
temptation to despair.

> *I give up! The LORD has added sorrow to my troubles. I am*
> *worn out from groaning, and I can't find any rest!*

We recall Jeremiah's own temptation to give up, to which
Yahweh replied that he had to pull himself together, for there
was worse to come (11:18-12:6). His reply to Baruch is
similar.

> *I, the LORD, am tearing down what I have built and pulling*
> *up what I have planted. I will do this to the entire earth.*
> *Are you looking for special treatment for yourself? Don't*
> *do it. I am bringing disaster on all mankind, but you will at*
> *least escape with your life, wherever you go. I, the LORD,*
> *have spoken (45:3-5 GNB).*

'You share Jeremiah's response to me. But this will not gain you exemption from the fate of the nation as a whole. You are identified with the true Israel, and that is great. But you cannot escape being identified also with the fate of the outward Israel. I promise you that your life will be preserved, as Jeremiah's will be. But you have to go through the fall of Jerusalem and the exile. The remnant does not escape the fate of the whole people. It is identified with them.'

Yet as Jeremiah and Baruch suffer, their suffering has a different meaning from that of the people as a whole. They do not suffer for their sins, but for the sins of others. And because they were willing to suffer, others can be blessed and brought nearer to God. Because Jeremiah was willing to suffer, and because Baruch was willing to suffer through being associated with Jeremiah, their lives and their words spoke to their own people. The very existence of Jeremiah's book is an evidence of that. Indeed, if *we* learn from the book of Jeremiah, if it takes us nearer to God and deeper into God, then this is because Jeremiah and Baruch were willing to accept the cost of bringing this book to birth, in being identified both with the true Israel of the promise, and with the outward Israel in its sin and punishment. So we gain through their affliction. But we are also challenged to be ready to accept it ourselves.

It may be that we cannot see ourselves as Jeremiahs. There was something unique about God's dealings with him: he was a prophet. It is more difficult to escape seeing oneself as Baruch. He is the ordinary man who responds to God's word. But his experience hints that there is not, after all, such a difference between what God expects of the 'ordinary' believer and how he deals with him, and what he expects of, and how he deals with, the prophet. Jeremiah embodies what it means to be Israel; Baruch embodies the required response to this, of being willing to walk the same way. And this response is the calling of all God's people. What happens to Jeremiah *is* what happens to the true Israel of God, and if we wish to be associated with the Israel of God then this is what we must accept. Being a prophet involves that identification. But the suffering, the identification, does bear fruit. It contributes to the history of the people of God.

IDENTIFICATION WITH YAHWEH

Jeremiah, we have suggested, is identified with Israel in his anguish, in his praying, and in his suffering. But he is identified also with God himself, and this further identification manifests itself in similar connections.

Jeremiah is identified with God in his anguish, as he is with Israel in hers. We may return once again to the first of the passages in which Jeremiah wrestles with the cost of being a prophet. Jeremiah's lament (11:18-12:6) is followed by what one can only describe as God's own lament.

> *I have forsaken the house of Israel,*
> *I have cast off my own people.*
> *I have given my beloved into the power of her foes.*
> *My people have turned on me like a lion from the scrub,*
> *roaring against me ...*
> *Many shepherds have ravaged my vineyard*
> *and trampled down my field,*
> *they have made my pleasant field a desolate wilderness,*
> *made it a waste land, waste and waterless, to my sorrow.*
> *The whole land is waste, and no one cares*
> *(12:7-8,10-11 NEB).*

Here is the anguish of God. Part of his response to Jeremiah's lament is to share his own. Jeremiah had asked whether God really cared about how Jeremiah felt and about how Israel was hell-bent on self-destruction. One element in God's response is to ask, 'How do you think I feel? Do you think I am a block of stone? Do you think I do not care? Do you think it does not break me, to forsake my house, to surrender my beloved to her enemies?' Jeremiah is invited into the anguish of God.

The same note is sounded in the prayers we referred to above.

> *Hope of Israel,*
> *its saviour in time of distress,*
> *why are you like a stranger in the land,*
> *like a traveller pitching his tent for a night? (14:8).*

Here is a telling description of God, a stranger in his own country, a homeless vagabond, a tramp.

> Let my eyes stream with tears
> day and night, without ceasing,
> for my maiden daughter, my people,
> is shattered and broken ... (14:17).

Here again is Jeremiah sharing the anguish of God. Indeed, it is a puzzle to decide whose anguish is referred to here. Are we reading about God's feelings (as in chapter 12)? Or of Jeremiah's? Von Rad (*Old Testament Theology* Volume 2, p.193) notes that in Jeremiah the distinction between God's words and the prophet's words becomes obscured. We are not sure whether we are reading lyrical poetry or the word of the Lord. But the reason why we cannot tell whether we are sharing Jeremiah's anguish or God's is that both are the same thing, because Jeremiah is identified with God. Jeremiah is torn apart not merely because of his own affliction, nor only because of Israel's affliction, but because of the affliction of God, which God allows him to share.

Jeremiah was also identified with Israel in his prayer. At this same point he is called to be identified with God, too. The record of his prayer is consequently an awesome dialogue between Jeremiah, the voice of Israel, and Jeremiah, the voice of God. He prays on Israel's behalf (14:7-9); but here is God's response:

> These are Yahweh's words to this people: They like their feet to wander, they exercise no control over them. But Yahweh does not accept them. He will now keep their wrong-doing in mind; he will punish their sins (14:10).

In the Old Testament, it was assumed that prayers would be answered. People poured out their sufferings and their longings and their needs before God, and prophet or priest in God's name declared God's response, his promise of blessing and forgiveness and restoration. But here in Jeremiah it is not that response. *Yahweh does not accept them. He will now keep their wrongdoing in mind*. Indeed, Jeremiah goes on,

> *Yahweh said to me, Do not pray for the well-being of this*
> *people. When they fast, I will not listen to their cry; when*
> *they offer whole-offering and grain-offering, I will not*
> *accept them (14:11-12).*

A prophet's task is to pray for his people, because he is identified with them. But sometimes, because he is also identified
with God, he has to take 'No' for an answer. The point is re-
asserted in the verses that follow. Jeremiah again prays on his
people's behalf, acknowledging their sin, pointing out their
needs, testifying to the Lordship of Yahweh, pleading for his
mercy (14:19-22). But the response is the same. Indeed, it is
perhaps more chilling.

> *Yahweh said to me, Even if Moses and Samuel stood*
> *before me, I would feel nothing for this people (15:1).*

Suppose these two great men of prayer, representatives res-
pectively of the Law and the Prophets, were at this moment
to rise from the dead and plead for Israel: their prayers would
not be heard.

Here Jeremiah's terrible gift of insight is to see when prayers
cannot be answered. Perhaps it is that he can see when
prayers are not real and when repentance is not genuine even
though the words are quite right. He can see when God's
people are past repentance and there is no escape from judgement and no way of averting disaster. And therefore he cannot pray. He cannot ask for the morally impossible. He has to
accept identification with God's will. He shares God's longing
that prayer should be answered, and also God's realization
that it cannot be. He shares God's anguish, but God also
allows (indeed requires) him to share God's indignation. *I*
have not kept the company of jokers and enjoyed myself.
Because your hand has been upon me, I have lived in isola-
tion, because you have filled me with indignation (15:17).
Jeremiah is distinct from the crowd because he is identified
with God in his anger as well as in his anguish. That was why
he held himself aloof from the roisterous merrymaking of his
contemporaries. It was incompatible with the divine indignation that filled him.

I am full of the anger of the LORD,
I cannot hold it in.
I must pour it out on the children in the street
and on the young men in their gangs.
Man and wife alike shall be caught in it,
the greybeard and the very old.
Their houses shall be turned over to others,
their fields and their women alike.
For I will raise my hand, says the LORD,
against the people of the country ... (6:11-12 NEB).

God feels anguish for his people (and presumably that makes
him long to answer their prayers), but he also feels anger for
them (and that means their prayers cannot be answered). The
remarkable tension felt by Jeremiah is attributed also to God
himself. Israel is his people, so he is attached to her. But she is
rebellious, so he is determined to punish her. She is his
beloved, and he loves her and grieves over her suffering. But
she is an adulteress, and he hates her and has no desire to
have her back. We are again reminded of Hosea, who in his
own life knew the tension between longing to abandon his
wife because she was unfaithful to him and being unable to
do so because she was his wife. That is God's position, and
Jeremiah's identification with God is an identification with
him in the ambiguity of his relationship with his people.

A final aspect of Jeremiah's identification with God to
which we may draw attention is that what men do to him is
what they do to God. We may come back to the question of
why these accounts of Jeremiah's affliction are in the Bible.
Some reasons we have suggested already. Jeremiah wrote
them down to give expression to the inner anguish which in
his public ministry he had to hide; and Jeremiah (or his followers) believed them to embody what it means to be the
people of God, to be the remnant, to be the suffering servant.
Yet Jeremiah suffers not merely because he is identified with
Israel, but also because he is identified with *God*. To be God
is to experience rejection and hostility, attack and crucifixion.
Whenever men can find God in his weakness, they crucify
him: from the blood of Abel to the blood of Zechariah (Luke
11:51).

So Jeremiah comes to his people as the representative of

God, and quite naturally he is crucified. That is perhaps why
we are told so many stories about the outward afflictions of
Jeremiah in the second half of the book. It is not because
someone was interested in writing Jeremiah's biography. It is
because what men were doing to Jeremiah they were doing to
God and his word. Jehoiakim dramatically consigns Jeremiah's scroll line by line into the fire—snip ... snip ... snip
(Jer. 36). That is what he did to God's word. And that essentially is what people tried to do to Jeremiah himself over the
years. Because Jeremiah is identified with God. He does not
talk about what is done to him because *he* is important, but
because it reveals something about God. His life and how he
is treated exhibits people's attitude to the word. What men do
to Jeremiah reflects what they think of God. God himself is
the God who suffers, the one who is pushed out of his world
onto a cross. He is the crucified God. So in Jeremiah we begin
to get a hint of a claim that will be developed in the vision of
the suffering servant, that in the affliction of his servant the
arm of the Lord is revealed (Isa. 53:1). Jeremiah's life witnesses
to this, through his identification with God.

CHAPTER THREE

What distinguishes a prophet?

To the modern reader, 'the prophets' generally mean well-known great Old Testament figures such as Elijah and Elisha, Amos and Hosea, Isaiah and Micah, Jeremiah and Ezekiel. Our acceptance of the Hebrew Scriptures decides for us who are *the* prophets.

For people living in the time of these men, however, matters were more complicated. They were not, in fact, the only 'prophets'; the Old Testament refers to many others, though without telling us much about them. Sometimes their names and their words have not survived because they did not have the deep significance that was found in the stories and the messages of *the* prophets. They were honourable, worthy men, used by God, but ultimately belonging to that vast army of the faithful whose names are known to God but not to historians. Others of them, however, were men who were quite opposed to the work of prophets such as Jeremiah. They brought a different message. The issues raised by this phenomenon have a prominent place in the book of Jeremiah; distinguishing an authentic prophet from a counterfeit prophet was an important issue in the period in which he lived.

JEREMIAH AND HANANIAH

A story relating to the last years of the independent life of Judah illustrates the questions that were being raised.

The nation of Israel had never been a major power in the world she belonged to, except for a short period in the time of David and Solomon. Usually she was under the authority of one of the bigger nations which commanded empires in the Middle East—Egypt or Assyria before the exile, in subsequent centuries Persia or Greece (Rome or Byzantium, Britain or America ...). During the time of Jeremiah, power in Mesopotamia passed from the Assyrians to the Babylonians. The time of transition was naturally a time of upheaval. The Babylonians more than once had to suppress attempts to throw off their authority at the edges of their empire. After one such attempt on the part of Judah, in 597 the Babylonians removed King Jehoiachin (Jeconiah) from the throne, and took him back to Babylonia, along with many of the other Judaean leaders and some of the temple vessels. They replaced Jehoiachin as king by their own nominee, Jehoiachin's uncle Zedekiah. But Zedekiah was a feeble leader, easily pushed this way or that. He was soon under pressure from within Judah and from the other vassal states in the area (Edom, Moab, Ammon, and so on) to rebel against the Babylonians once again.

At this time, Jeremiah sent messages to Zedekiah to the effect that there ought to be no rebellion against Babylon. It is Yahweh who has given power over the area to Nebuchadrezzar, the Babylonian king. His authority ought to be accepted until Yahweh takes it away from him again. The Judaeans, in particular, are not to listen to voices declaring that the vessels of Yahweh's house, the temple of Solomon, would soon be returned. On the contrary, if Judah does not submit, she will lose the rest of the treasured vessels and fitments of the temple, and indeed will lose her very land itself as she is taken off to join Jehoiachin in exile (Jer. 27).

Jeremiah's words were in direct conflict, however, with those of another prophet, named Hananiah. Hananiah declared that Yahweh would indeed soon bring the temple vessels back to Jerusalem. The Babylonian yoke would be broken (Jer. 28:1-11).

So who is the authentic prophet? How are people to decide this? What are the marks of a true prophet which differentiate him from a false prophet? As we look back on the story of Jeremiah at the time of this confrontation with Hananiah, it is easy to know whose side we are on. It is quite clear who is the goody, who the baddy. History has passed its verdict. But that was not the case for people living at the time.

There is often a similar difficulty about evaluating the alleged prophets of our own age. There are many 'prophetic' figures in the world today: those who declare that the world, or particular societies, or particular institutions are on the wrong track and must radically reconsider what they are doing. There is the conservation movement; the anti-psychiatry movement (R. D. Laing, Thomas Szasz); the anti-education movement (Ivan Illich). There are many 'prophetic' movements within the church: liberation theology; various voices in the World Council of Churches; and, of course, nearer home for many people, those who claim 'the gift of prophecy' or similar gifts and proclaim in congregational worship that 'this is the word of the Lord'. How do we tell which *are* the words of the Lord?

There were apparently no outward differences between Jeremiah and Hananiah. Both exercised a public ministry in the temple before the priests and people. Both prophesied in the name of Yahweh: 'Thus says Almighty Yahweh, the God of Israel.' Both stood in respectable Israelite traditions. Jeremiah might remind one of Hosea, as we have seen, or of Micah (in chapter 26 it is the similarity of Jeremiah's gloomy message to Micah's that leads to his escaping being lynched for speaking of God's judgement on Jerusalem). But Hananiah in turn might remind one of Deuteronomy (which promised that a people that reformed herself, as in some ways Judah had in the time of Josiah, would be blessed by God) and of Isaiah (who had in his day promised the deliverance of Jerusalem in terms quite similar to those used by Hananiah).

Both Jeremiah and Hananiah used 'symbolic actions'. Jeremiah made his preaching concrete by putting on the ox-yoke (the ball and chain, as it were) that Judah was destined for. Hananiah made his preaching concrete by breaking these.

There was apparently no difference between Jeremiah and other prophets in the unusual behaviour that they exhibited when they were (allegedly) in touch with God. Jeremiah 29 speaks of the high priest having authority over every madman who prophesies—and the category includes Jeremiah (29:26-7). Now it is the case that Jeremiah does not speak of the 'spirit' coming on him (a phrase which suggests a special experience of the power and presence of God which often made a man act in abnormal ways) as earlier and later prophets do (e.g. 2 Kings 2; Ezek. 11). But apparently his contemporaries did not notice a difference here. One may note a Christian parallel in the use of tongues and other gifts outside the Christian community, or within it but for the glory of lords other than Jesus (1 Cor. 12:2-3). There is no outward difference in the exercise of the gift.

There is no apparent difference in the means by which the prophet claims to receive his message. Jeremiah has visions (e.g. Jer. 1; 4:19-31), and so do the other prophets (23:16). Jeremiah has dreams (31:26); so do the other prophets (23:27-8).

Perhaps, then, being in truth entrusted with God's word gives a prophet a special boldness or conviction, so that his manner or his bearing is somehow different from those of the man who has no real commission from God? Apparently not. When Hananiah broke the symbolic ox-yoke from Jeremiah's neck and declared that Yahweh was about to break the Babylonian yoke from the nation's neck in the same way (Jer. 28: 10-11), it is Hananiah who seems to have the real authority. He has the last word. And Jeremiah the prophet *goes his way*: tail between his legs, defeated again. We are once more reminded of the Paul of 2 Corinthians, derided as a time-server, good at writing letters but poor at face-to-face confrontation, unimpressive in the cut-and-thrust of argument (2 Cor. 10:10), rather feeble compared with the real apostles the Corinthians are enthralled by.

Now in the end, though Hananiah won this battle of words (and of symbolic actions), it was a costly victory. The chilling final verses of the story (Jer. 28:12-17) relate how Jeremiah declares sentence of death on Hananiah for *uttering rebellion against Yahweh*; and within two months Hananiah is dead.

But at the time of the confrontation, one might have been hard put to it to decide whether Hananiah or Jeremiah was nearer to the mind of Yahweh. So what does distinguish an authentic prophet?

'CONCERNING THE PROPHETS'

Clearly this question will have been of huge importance to Jeremiah. His own attempts to identify what was wrong with the other prophets are collected most systematically in a section of his book headed, *'Concerning the prophets'* (Jer. 23:9-40).

His analysis opens with a spirited lament at what might be called their moral and theological relativism: they fail to maintain God's standards with regard to ethics and with regard to faith. Jeremiah begins by describing one of those moments of anguish and indignation which we referred to earlier. Yahweh has spoken his holy words, and they have a devastating effect on Jeremiah himself. *My heart is broken within me, all my bones shake* (23:9 RSV). Probably both those phrases are misleading in English. The ' heart ' in Hebrew thinking refers to the seat of intelligence and decision making. Later, Jeremiah speaks of the false prophets' *visions of their own minds* and of the intentions of God's *mind* (23:16,20), and in both places it is the Hebrew word for 'heart' that is used. At the beginning of his lament, then, he is not referring to the breaking of his heart (in our sense) but to the blowing of his mind. And his bones shaking is another way of expressing the same thing—I was shattered, we might say. God has brought home to him the enormity of what is going on in Judah. The calamities they experience have come upon them because of the immorality and injustice which abound: *the land is full of adulterers ... Their speed is in doing evil and their strength is in doing what is not right* (23:10). Furthermore, *prophet and priest* are just as involved as anyone, and their wrongdoing takes place even in the temple itself (23:11). They follow the people in their sin, instead of leading them from it. This is the first element in Jeremiah's indictment of the other prophets.

The second element in their moral and theological relativism links with this. They encourage adultery and deceit rather than turning people from it. The prophets of the northern kingdom in the old days were bad enough. They led Israel astray, encouraging her to worship the Canaanite baals (23:13). Their theology was manifestly unorthodox. But there is a sense in which the theology Jeremiah finds among his fellow prophets in Jerusalem is even more twisted. They prophesy in the name of Yahweh, the holy God, and in his name they encourage evil. What Jeremiah sees is not merely *unsavoury* (23:13) but *repulsive* (23:14).

The prophets of Jerusalem are failing, in fact, at a point at which the Torah warns that prophets may fail. Deuteronomy twice discusses the significance of prophecy and the problem of distinguishing true from false prophecy. The succession of prophets would be God's way of providing the guidance his people needed, which in Moses' day they received from Moses himself (18:15-19). But a prophet who leads Israel after other gods, encouraging 'wickedness' and 'rebellion' against Yahweh, is to be put to death (13:1-11). Thus Jeremiah declares that the prophets *strengthen the hands of evildoers, so that no one turns from his wickedness*; and therefore they will forfeit their lives (Jer. 23:14-15). He declares judgement on Hananiah because he has encouraged *rebellion* (28:16: the same rare Hebrew word is used here and in Deut. 13:5—and also in Jer. 29:32).

So Jeremiah claims that by their attitude the prophets cut themselves off from the company of those who take the Torah seriously. They are working against it.

Further, the other prophets preach empty hope instead of unpleasant truth. They are *filling you with false hopes ... They are continually saying, 'All will go well with you', to people who despise Yahweh's word. They say to anyone who follows the inclinations of his own stubbornness, 'No trouble will come upon you'* (23:16,17). They say, 'It will be well with you'—*shalom* to you. As Jeremiah has put it earlier, *They have treated my people's wound superficially, saying 'All will be well, all will be well'—when it will not* (6:14; 8:11). There is no *shalom*; but they say, *shalom, shalom*. In order to emphasize the quality of something in Hebrew, often the word itself will be repeated. The song of songs is the best song; holy, holy, holy (repeating the word three times) is *ultimate* holiness. Thus shalom, shalom is perfect peace. ' Thou dost keep him in perfect peace, whose mind is stayed on thee', Isaiah says (26:3 RSV): thou dost keep him in *shalom shalom*. But in the time of Jeremiah *shalom shalom* is the promise of the false prophets. The characteristic word of the true prophet, Jeremiah claims, is that there is trouble to come. Jeremiah reminds Hananiah that their predecessors had generally spoken of *war, famine, and plague* (28:8). So Hananiah and the other prophets of Jeremiah's day stand outside the authentic prophetic tradition, as well as beyond the Torah.

Now of course the prophet's motive in declaring a word of judgement was a positive one. His aim was to bring people to repentance. He was trying to be constructive. The other prophets *look* as if they are being constructive. They appear to be trying to build up the people's faith, hope and confidence. But Ezekiel, in his discussion of false prophecy (Ezek. 13), offers two vivid descriptions of them. They look as if they are strengthening Israel. Actually they are only whitewashing a wall (papering over the cracks, we would say); and wall-paper and whitewash will not stop it collapsing. Or they are like foxes scavenging among ruins, instead of people who have seriously gone up into the breaches or built up a wall for the house of Israel. When the day of Yahweh's anger comes, the wall will collapse. Their constructive-*looking* ministry is destructive in *effect*. What is needed is to bring Israel to her senses. That is why the characteristic word of a true prophet is a word of judgement.

The characteristic word, that is. Jeremiah does speak of hope for the future. He promises that a branch will grow from the tree of David which is being cut down, a righteous branch; and a new exodus will take the people out of the bondage that is coming, and will eclipse the memory of the first exodus (23:5-8). He promises a restoration of the joy that is being taken away and the establishing of a better relationship between God and his people than they enjoyed under the old covenant. He promises *shalom*, in fact (29:11; 33:6). But it is to be peace after conflict, restoration after judgement; no peace without chastisement and repentance.

There, then, are three characteristics of false prophecy; their opposites will characterize true prophecy. If the false prophets followed the people in their sin instead of leading them from it, then a true prophet will be one whose own life is an embodiment of God's truth. He will be a man who is capable of standing out from the vices of his contemporaries, even of the rest of God's people. If someone brings 'prophetic' words, but his own life is no better than average, we may be suspicious of his prophecy. As was the case with Jeremiah, a prophet's life is part of his message.

Then, if the false prophets encouraged adultery and deceit instead of resisting it, an authentic prophet will be one who brings home God's moral demands. He will be one who perceives where people are ignoring God's standards and where they despise his word. For God's people delude themselves just as unbelievers do. They become blind to aspects of God's teaching, fool themselves that they are living committed lives, and produce sophisticated rationalizations for sin. Often the next generation can see it, but part of the blindness is that one cannot see it in oneself. Here is where the people of God always need prophets, who will enable us to break through the blindness and deafness of our particular cultural relativity.

Again, if the false prophets offered vain hopes instead of unpleasant truth, then a true prophet is one who dares say what goes against the grain, what will not be welcome. Contemporary 'charismatic' prophecy tends to be encouraging and reassuring. But in Jeremiah's day the promise of God's presence and his love was the message of the false prophets.

Admittedly doom is not always God's word through his prophets. Much of the books of Isaiah and Ezekiel, and (as we have noted) some of Jeremiah's own words, concerned hope for the future. But even here words of comfort and consolation are tied up in different ways with words of judgement; there is no papering over cracks. Furthermore, in each situation a prophet is confronting the attitudes of those to whom he speaks. Even the message of peace is one that confronts, rather than colludes with, the attitudes of those the prophet has to address. Isaiah speaks of the possibility of trusting in

the power and the promises of Yahweh, but speaks to people
who do not want to believe in these and are inclined to rely
on political stratagems. Ezekiel and Isaiah 40-55 speak of restoration for the exiles, but speak to people who do not wish
to be lifted from the morass of depression and doubt into
which the reality of God's judgement has taken them. Haggai
and Zechariah declare that the temple will be rebuilt, but
address people who no longer believe that Yahweh will fulfil
his promises and have abandoned attempts to live as if he is
going to. Whether it is words of judgement or words of hope,
prophecy is confrontational and is addressed to the specific
circumstances in which the prophet finds himself. So the real
prophet is the one who is prepared to confront and who is
able to tell whether this is a day of judgement or a day of
hope.

In these ways, then, authentic prophecy resists moral and
theological relativism. The other major feature of Jeremiah's
critique of the prophets is that their words have no origin
outside themselves. The point is made negatively by describing where their messages did not come from. They have not
stood in Yahweh's council to see and hear his word (23:18).
Yahweh's council is the heavenly equivalent to the bishop's
council or the parish council or the county council. It is the
place where decisions are made about policy, strategy and
action in heaven, and on earth. The Old Testament includes
several vivid descriptions of it: Yahweh and the sons of God
discussing the spirituality of Job (Job 1-2); Yahweh and the
host of heaven determining judgement on Ahab (1 Kings 22);
God holding judgement on the 'gods' themselves in the divine
council (Ps. 82); Yahweh commissioning his agents to begin
the process of comforting his people, these agents declaring
that Yahweh's way home to Palestine is to be prepared, a
voice commissioning the prophet himself to preach to the
exiles despite the despair he shares with them (Isa. 40). The
privilege of a prophet is to be allowed to listen to the debate
in this heavenly council. But *who has stood in Yahweh's
council to see and hear his word? Who has paid attention to
my word and heard it*? (23:18). The only person of whom
that can be true is the person who declares a message of judgement, the one who speaks of storm and wrath, of tempest

and anger (23:19-20). Those are the plans that are being formulated in heaven.

How does Jeremiah know? He knows in his own heart, ultimately, only because he believes he *has* stood in Yahweh's council. That is just part of his experience. He cannot prove that it was real; experience cannot be validated like that. He can describe it, but he cannot prove its authenticity. Men in general can talk about their deepest spiritual experiences, but we cannot thereby prove the validity of what we testify to. The experiences have to be real to us; Jeremiah's experience is truly the foundation of his ministry. But he cannot communicate the nature of his experience in such a way as to prove its authenticity.

So how were people to know that Jeremiah's message was true? One test, though it is little help when the prophecy is delivered, is the test of time. *Yahweh's anger will not turn aside until he has completely accomplished the intentions of his mind. In time you will understand this clearly* (23:20). History will prove Jeremiah right. Like Isaiah (see Isa. 8:16), Jeremiah wrote down his prophecies so that they could be checked against events in due course. They will be there on record when the moment of truth comes.

Jeremiah's prophecies came to be put together after his ministry was over and he had been proved to be in the right over the fall of Jerusalem. This seems to have been a period when there was a crisis over prophecy; so much prophecy had been discredited by the collapse of the state. We need to keep recalling that, although with hindsight we know this was only false prophecy, at the time it was just prophecy— full stop. Authentic and false prophecy were difficult to distinguish. So it was prophecy itself that was in danger of being discredited. Furthermore, there was thus a danger that the real word of the Lord would be ignored. At this point, in the exile, the test of fulfilment was very important. Certainly most prophecy had been discredited. But the person who is genuinely seeking God's word will not let the true be lost with the false.

The church in subsequent centuries has several times had to deal with excess and falsehood proclaimed in the name of the spirit of prophecy. This happened in Corinth; it happened

with the Montanists. In the latter case, the catholic church
stifled Montanism and drove it out of the church. Paul's own
approach, however, was to deal firmly with excess, but to
strive *not* to quench the Spirit. Long before, Jewish leaders in
the exile were doing the same: they acknowledged that prophecy had gone wrong, but urged attention to that prophecy
which had been in truth the Lord's word and had now been
vindicated by events. That they succeeded is evidenced by
the fact that the author of Isaiah 40-55 can appeal to the fulfilled prophecies of before the exile (*earlier things have clearly
come about*) and build on them by *declaring fresh things*
(42:9). His promises are very like those of the false prophets
that Jeremiah condemns, but they are distinct from them
because they begin by affirming that judgement had indeed
been God's word at that point. There is a certain value, then,
in seeking to distinguish true from false by whether it comes
true.

So Jeremiah's first distinguishing mark which characterizes
what is true over against what is false is the mark of religious
experience: the true prophet has stood in Yahweh's council.
But that cannot be seen. The second is that a prophet's words
find fulfilment. But that cannot be seen until it happens. The
third mark takes us back to the point made earlier in this collection of material on prophecy. *I did not send the prophets;
it was they who ran. I did not speak to them; it was they who
prophesied. If they had stood in my council, they would have
proclaimed my words to my people. They would have turned
them from the utterly evil course on which they are engaged*
(23:21-22). The visible mark of prophecy is, does the prophet
turn people away from their evil way? Does he follow them
in sin or lead them from it? Does he encourage adultery and
deceit or resist it? Does he offer vain hope or unpleasant
truth? The person who has stood in Yahweh's council meets
the moral test, because he has been privy to the formulating
of a moral policy.

The message of other prophets did *not* come from having
stood in Yahweh's council. It came, to put the point positively, simply from themselves (23:23-32). Ask the prophets
themselves where they get their messages from. They relate
their dreams, for instance (23:25). Now in principle dreams

are a means of revelation which God can use. Joel promises a time when all sorts of people will dream dreams and see visions (Joel 2:28-29). But in these examples in Jeremiah's time, anyway, there is a world of difference between a man's dream and Yahweh's word. *So let the prophet who has a dream relate his dream, but let the one who has my word speak my word in truth* (23:28). Let us grant that dreams can be a means of the Lord's message coming, but today we see even more clearly than people may have done in Jeremiah's day that dreams are usually the means whereby our own subconscious finds expression. There is a world of difference between a man's dream and the Lord's word: the difference between straw and wheat; for the Lord's word is like fire, or like a hammer that can shatter rock (23:28,29).

The false prophets' messages come from their own mind. Jeremiah declares that as they *prophesy lies*, they *prophesy the deceptions of their own mind* (23:26); they *prophesy lies in my name* (23:25). To speak or act in God's name is to speak or act as God, as if you were God himself. It is to claim to be God's mouthpiece. The Jews came later to be so wary of a mistake when they took God's name on their lips that they avoided uttering God's name at all. At least they thereby recognized how solemn it is to speak of God. Jeremiah hears his contemporaries flaunting Yahweh's name but attaching it to their own thoughts.

Further, they derive their messages from each other (23:30). I recall some years ago going to a parish church and hearing a brilliant sermon from the curate on the promise that 'he who believes shall not make haste' (Isa. 28:16). A few weeks later, I found the sermon word for word in a book by John Robinson. Why should a man preach someone else's sermon? Because he was under pressure and did not have time to prepare one? This might be defensible, though arguably he ought to attribute it! Or was it because he had nothing to say? Presumably that was the case with the false prophets. They were not in touch with God; they were not privy to his council. But they had to say something. So they borrowed each other's sermons.

Again, the other prophets' words came from their own mouths: they *have only to move their tongues to utter oracles*

(23:31 JB). They have the gift of the gab. They will never be lost for words. That is a great gift. But one needs to recall that fluency does not prove that one is in touch with God. It means that if we do not receive words, we will be able to make them up. Jeremiah was aware from the beginning of not having this gift. *Lord Yahweh, I do not know how to speak* (1:6). When Hananiah contradicted him, Jeremiah had no answer. But at least it meant that when he did speak it was because he had Yahweh's words; he was not merely exercising his own big mouth.

The false prophets' messages came not from Yahweh's council, but from their own dreams, from their own minds, from each other, from their own mouths. Jeremiah's material *'concerning the prophets'* closes on a different note. *When this people, or a prophet or priest, ask you, 'What is the burden of Yahweh's message', you are to say to them, 'You are the burden, and I am going to get rid of you'* (23:33; the following verses develop the point). There was something profoundly wrong with the prophets. But there was also something profoundly wrong with their audience, and a congregation gets the prophets it deserves. You are the Lord's burden, says Jeremiah, with your frivolous attitude to God's word to you. So while we ought to be critical in our approach to prophecy, we also must be self-critical over our own attitude to the word of God.

WHAT MAKES A FALSE PROPHET?

Questions concerning the nature of true and false prophecy have aroused considerable interest in Old Testament study in recent years. In one of the books on this subject, *Prophetic Conflict: Its Effect upon Israelite Religion* (1971), James L. Crenshaw includes an analysis of why false prophecy was inevitable. 'Inevitable' is a discouraging word; it ought not to excuse us from a determination to resist the pressures that in Israel led to false prophecy. If we are willing to learn from history, we may be able to avoid repeating its mistakes.

One factor that influences a prophet to speak false rather than true is a desire for acceptance. A prophet wants to be right, but he also wants to be listened to. He may sincerely want both of these for God's sake. But both may not be possible; in Israel, indeed, they were regularly mutually exclusive. It is clear in Jeremiah's case (and even clearer in Isaiah 40-55) that God's servant makes his contribution to God's purpose by accepting failure and opposition. The desire to succeed, even to gain a hearing for God, can be the desire of the false prophet.

A second threat to authentic prophecy is the institution. In Israel this meant the monarchy. Now the great age of prophecy is the period of the monarchy. The first great prophet is Samuel, in the time of Saul, and the last prophets whose ministry we can explicitly date, Haggai and Zechariah, offer the Old Testament's last account of a Davidic prince's activity in Israel. Thus it was the monarchy that called forth prophecy. But prophecy's function in relation to the monarchy was to stand up to its attempts to absolutize its own position. Naturally, this stand would lead to attempts on the monarchy's part to stifle prophecy (as the story of Jeremiah illustrates). So the relationship between prophecy and the monarchy is paradoxical and ambivalent, and one of a prophet's temptations will be to subordinate his prophecy to the power of the monarchy. Another embodiment of the institution in Israel is the temple and its priesthood, and there is characteristically a further tension between organized religion and prophecy. The official pressure on Jeremiah to moderate his message (and thus to abandon authentic prophecy) comes from Pashhur in the temple as well as Jehoiakim in the palace.

The pressure of the temple leads us to a fourth threat to authentic prophecy, the power of popular religion. Sometimes this may be overtly syncretistic religion, such as the baalism Jeremiah opposes but of which he accuses other prophets. On other occasions it may be a faith which is Yahwistic in its outward expression. Hananiah prophesied in the name of Yahweh and picked up the emphases of popular religion: 'God is on our side, we shall overcome.' Popular religion is perhaps most often characterized by an easy optimism of this kind. But the exile marks the transition to another kind of popular religion, a widespread conviction that Yahweh has abandoned his people. It is this conviction that the later message of Ezekiel and that of Isaiah 40-55 has to combat. Here, too, the prophet may well be tempted to accede to popular conviction, which could sound very pious. But if he does so, he is an inauthentic prophet, because he has missed the transition from the day of judgement to the day of grace. The prophet has to be wary of both the optimism and the pessimism of popular religion.

Popular (Yahwistic) religion can take as its ally Yahwistic religious tradition. As we noted above, Hananiah's assurance that Yahweh would look after the fortunes of Judah was based on authentic streams of Israelite belief, the Psalms' commitment to David and to Zion which was emphasized also by Isaiah, and the promises of Deuteronomy that a nation that reformed itself would find a life of blessing. The trouble with Hananiah was only that his message belonged to the previous century. He let himself be led astray because he found something in what was authentic tradition, in the past words of God but it led him into inauthentic prophecy.

Crenshaw's final reason for the development of false prophecy was the increasing stress on the individual which characterized the period of the exile. This raised more sharply the question of whether God treats individuals with justice, and leads to the temptation to try to justify the ways of God with men, and perhaps encouraged some prophets to promise peace because trouble would be unfair to those within the nation who were faithful to God.

The pressures upon a prophet are such that it may not only be inevitable that there are false prophets; it may also be unavoidable that a prophet (such as Jeremiah) whose basic commitment is to the truth nevertheless sometimes falls into error. Certainly Jeremiah does so. But we shall see in the next chapter that this is not the end of the road for him.

CHAPTER FOUR

What makes a man a prophet?

So to be a prophet means being willing to accept the cost of serving God in this way. It means accepting the tension of a twofold identification, with God in his anguish and indignation, and with Israel in her anguish and high calling. It means to stand boldly in confrontation with men, without ever being quite able to prove that the words which you declare are ones which you have overheard in Yahweh's council. But what keeps Jeremiah to this task? How is it that he can find no escape from it?

JEREMIAH'S CALL

Several of the prophets tell us how they came to receive their prophetic calling. In the cases of Isaiah and Amos, the account comes in the midst of their books, but in each case at a significant point. Isaiah's (Isa. 6) marks the beginning of the story of the prophet's confrontation with King Ahaz, a battle to get king and people to take their God seriously in their political life. It is a battle Isaiah will lose, a time when he will look defeated. But he prefaces the story with the account of his call, as if to say, 'This is why my word is going to come true even though Ahaz ignores it, because my word has its origin in an occasion when I myself was confronted by God, the holy one of Israel, enthroned in heaven and worshipped by the host of heaven.'

It is the same with Amos (Amos 7). King Jeroboam's representative advises Amos that he would be wise to publish his declarations of judgement on Jeroboam in a less indiscreet location than Jeroboam's personal royal chapel at Bethel. 'Whose idea do you think it was that I came here?', asks Amos. 'Do you think I enjoy risking my life? I did not choose to be a prophet. I was not brought up in the vicarage. The Lord took me, the Lord sent me.'

When Jeremiah and Ezekiel tell us at the beginning of their books how they became prophets, their accounts also provide the background and the justification for the prophecies that follow. We may imagine Jeremiah standing on the temple mount or in the Damascus Gate at Jerusalem, where people gathered for trade and gossip and judicial proceedings. 'This is the word of the Lord', he says. Listen for the responses of the shopkeepers in the gate: 'O, come on Jeremiah, why should we believe you?' Watch the priests in their huddles: 'This man is anti-Israelite, he is dangerous, he will have to be dealt with.' As he hears those responses to his preaching, it is the account of how the Lord commissioned him to be a prophet that comes back to Jeremiah. He is supported in and kept to his prophetic task because in the thirteenth year of the reign of Josiah the son of Amon, King of Judah (626 BC), Yahweh spoke to him.

> Yahweh's word came to me:
>   'Before I formed you in the womb, I acknowledged you;
>   before you were born, I set you apart;
>   I appointed you as a prophet to the nations.'
> I said,
>   'But sovereign Yahweh, I do not know how to speak.
>   I am only a young man.'
> But Yahweh said to me,
>   'Do not say, "I am only a young man",
>   because you are to go to anyone to whom I send you,
>   and to say anything that I tell you.

> *Do not be afraid of them,*
> *because I will be with you to keep you safe.*
> *This is Yahweh's message.'*
> Then Yahweh put out his hand, touched my mouth, and
> said to me,
> *'I have put my words in your mouth.*
> *Today I have appointed you over nations and kingdoms,*
> *to uproot and to demolish,*
> *to destroy and to overthrow,*
> *to build and to plant (1:4-10).*

Four moments or aspects of Jeremiah's calling as a prophet
may perhaps be distinguished here. Jeremiah begins by recalling, 'Yahweh chose me'. As the Lord actually put it, *I
acknowledged you*. Jeremiah uses the ordinary verb for 'to
know', which generally means just the same in Hebrew as it
does in English—I know my wife, I know the date, I know
the English language. But sometimes in the Old Testament
(especially in the prophets), it means something more. Jeremiah himself speaks of people not knowing God's standards
of conduct (5:4-5), and he means not merely that they were
not acquainted with the law, but that they did not acknowledge the law. To know is to acknowledge, to recognize, to
commit oneself to. It involves the will as well as the understanding. Again, in Amos God says to Israel, 'You only have
I known of all the families of the earth' (Amos 3:2). Not that
God was unaware of the existence of the other nations, but he
was uniquely committed to Israel.

So it was between God and Jeremiah. God knew Jeremiah
before he was born. He took notice of him. He thought about
him. He acknowledged him as his own. *Before I formed you
in the womb*. Jeremiah no doubt knew quite well where
babies came from. But here he ignores the human agency involved in reproduction, like the psalmist who recalls that
God knit him together in his mother's womb (Ps. 139:13).
The same agent who was responsible for Jeremiah existing at
all was responsible for his call to God's service. '*I* formed you
in the womb—but before even that, *I* knew you. I acknowledged you, I committed myself to you.' The God who was
destining him for a certain sphere of service was Lord of
every experience that came to him even before his call, even

when he was in the womb. *Before you were born I set you apart*, designated you for a specific, particular role. Jeremiah's words were picked up by Paul and used to describe his call: God set him apart before he was born (Gal. 1:15).

In particular, God says, *I appointed you as a prophet to the nations*. The words that Yahweh was to give him were ones that referred not merely to individuals and their private lives, not even merely to the whole people of God. They involved the international powers. If Jeremiah was to bring any serious message to Judah in his day, it had to involve politics and international affairs. Individualistic piety was not enough; God's concerns were wider than that. So the man with God's message finds himself saying things that involve the nations. It can be dangerous enough (or at least potentially humiliating) to confront the people of God with what you claim is God's message. To speak of political and national affairs can be even more uncomfortable. But Jeremiah can look back on Yahweh's saying, *I appointed you as a prophet to the nations*.

So here is a man who has not yet been born. But God has given his mind to Jeremiah, committed himself to him, set him apart for a particular task, and given him a role with an international significance which God could foresee in his total purpose. *I acknowledged you ... I set you apart ... I appointed you ...* This is where Jeremiah would begin when asked, 'Why should we believe you?'. The answer is, 'Yahweh chose me.'

Then, he would go on, 'Yahweh called me.' The Lord's choice becomes the Lord's call when he puts his choice into words to the man he has in mind, and it is this experience that Jeremiah recalls in the opening chapter of his book. There was a specific moment to which Jeremiah could look back, when he heard God's voice telling him what his place in God's purpose was.

The Bible and Christian history are full of stories of how particular individuals were called to particular roles in God's service. The experiences have a concreteness about them which makes them different from anything that happens to many people today, and we wonder whether the experience was real. Indeed, perhaps the shopkeepers in the gate responded rather sceptically to Jeremiah. 'Come on, Jeremiah, how do you know you were not fooling yourself? Lots of un-balanced people think they have been called by God!' Perhaps Jeremiah anticipated that objection, because something he tells us about his call and about his reaction to the Lord's words to him speaks to this hypothetical question. *I said, 'But sovereign Yahweh, I do not know how to speak, I am only a young man.'* How old Jeremiah actually was we do not know; but the reaction tells us how old (or rather how young) he felt. 'Lord, I'm not experienced enough, I'm not wise enough, I haven't had the training. I read the message of Isaiah or Micah, I listen to the confident sermons of contemporary prophets, and I feel I can't compete with that.'

This was Jeremiah's reaction to God's call. So later, when questioned or challenged, he can look back on it and say, 'I did not want to be a prophet. Indeed I often think even now I wish I were not. I tried to get out of the task. But the Lord overcame my *unwillingness*. The Lord called me.'

Yahweh's response to Jeremiah's hesitation is to remind him that he will give Jeremiah the words to speak. *Do not say, 'I am only a young man', because you are to go to anyone to whom I send you, and to say anything that I tell you* (1:7). The theme is continued subsequently: *Yahweh put out his hand, touched my mouth, and said to me, 'I have put my words in your mouth'* (1:9). At the beginning of his ministry God gives Jeremiah a message that he is to deliver throughout the years that follow. But also throughout that ministry God will carry on giving him his words: *You are to say anything that I tell you.*

It would indeed be a demanding calling to have the right words for all those situations and people that Jeremiah had to address: the right words for people whose eyes seemed to be shut to God's truth and which he longed to be a means of the Lord's opening so that they could see the truth and respond to it; the right words for people like Baruch who did respond— words of encouragement or challenge, of reassurance or rebuke; the right words for the authorities with which he had to deal. How could a man have the right words in all these circumstances? *Sovereign Yahweh, I do not know how to speak ... You are to say anything that I tell you ... I have put my words in your mouth.*

There is one further element in Jeremiah's recollection of his call to which we should draw attention. Consider again those priests in the temple court plotting to dispose of Jeremiah. Here, too, the account of his call has something to say. 'The Lord protects me.' *Do not be afraid of them, because I will be with you to keep you safe. This is Yahweh's message* (1:8). There is a clear logical sequence about God's words here. First, *I am with you.* Here is one of the Bible's recurrent promises. 'The Lord of hosts is with us' (Ps. 46:7,11). 'His name shall be called Emmanuel (which means, God with us)' (Matt. 1:23). 'Lo, I am with you always' (Matt. 28:20). I am with you. Therefore, secondly, I will *keep you safe*. Whether it is from the hordes of foreign armies (as in Psalm 46), or from the power of sin (as in Matthew 1), or from the forces that oppose the gospel (as in Matthew 28), you will be delivered. Therefore, thirdly, *do not be afraid*. The sequence is completely logical. ' The Lord protects me.' But I suspect Jeremiah must have puzzled over those promises a few times. 'God is with me. He delivers me. I need not be afraid. That is what the promise says. So I get put in the stocks, lowered into a cistern, imprisoned in the court of the guard, and finally carted off into obscurity in Egypt. God is with me?' It sounds like the beginning to one of those Jewish jokes that are so profound in their acceptance of the trouble that it has meant to be a Jew: 'Lord, if this is what it means to have you *with* me, what is it like to have you *against* me?'

Yet somehow, it is true that the Lord is with Jeremiah to keep him safe. Jeremiah is the suffering prophet, the weeping prophet, the life and soul of the funeral. But that is a road he walks with God. *I will be with you, to keep you safe. So do not be afraid of them.* The Authorized Version has, 'be not afraid of their faces'. It may be an overtranslation, but nevertheless it's very true to Jeremiah. All the indications suggest that Jeremiah was not by nature a bombastic, confident extravert. He did not enjoy being a prophet; he tried to get out of it more than once. He did not like having to confront people. It was not his nature. All the more significant, then, is Yahweh's encouragement. Do not be afraid of their faces, or of their presence, or of having to confront them. Because I

will be with you to keep you safe. 'Yahweh chose me; Yahweh called me; Yahweh gives me the words to speak; Yahweh
keeps me safe.'

JEREMIAH'S RE-CALL

That would be a good note on which to conclude a considera-
tion of Jeremiah. Yet it would be a false note, because it might
in the end suggest something too easy. It is more appropriate
to conclude by returning to a passage from Jeremiah's laments.

> *Oh, no! My mother, why did you bear me,*
> *a man involved in strife and contention through the whole*
> *   land? ...*
> *Have I not interceded with you for the enemy*
> *when he was in trouble and distress?*
> *Yahweh, remember me, attend to me,*
> *avenge me on my persecutors!*
> *You are slow to anger, but do not let me be taken.*
> *Consider the insults I bear on your account.*
> *Your words came, and I accepted them;*
> *your words were my joy, the delight of my heart,*
> *because you had made me your own ...*
> *Why is my pain unceasing,*
> *my wound so severe, refusing to heal?*
> *You are just like a brook that fails,*
> *whose waters cannot be relied on   (15:10,11,15,16,18).*

'Before you were born, I set you apart'? *My mother, why did
you bear me?* 'I will be with you to keep you safe'? *Why is my
pain unceasing, my wound so severe, refusing to heal*? 'I have
put my words in your mouth'? Yes indeed, *your words came,
and I accepted them; your words were my joy, the delight of
my heart*. But their message does not come true: *You are just
like a brook that fails, whose waters cannot be relied on.* In
this lament Jeremiah seems to take up each element in his
memory of his call to be a prophet, and repudiate it. He
systematically tears to pieces the account of his call to
Yahweh's service.

   We may at this point note a contrast between Jeremiah and
Jesus. Jesus does not go back on God's call. In Gethsemane he

does query it, but he always accepts it. Jeremiah is more like
Jesus Christ Superstar, who accepts God's call because, as he
puts it, 'You hold all the cards.' There is something closer to
resignation or compulsion there. The tortured surrender of
Jeremiah or Jesus Christ Superstar contrasts with the willing
acceptance of God's will by the Jesus of the Gospels, who can
walk the tightrope of querying God's will without going back
on his commitment to it.

Jeremiah and Jesus also differ in their attitude to their
earthly enemies. Both pray for forgiveness for their persecutors. But here Jeremiah also prays for their punishment. In
itself that is not wrong; prayer for justice to be done is prayer
for God's will to be done. But the matter seems to have
become one of personal vengeance: *avenge me on my persecutors*. Jeremiah, in the end, breaks. It should not surprise us;
he *is* only a man. We will not make the mistake of pretending
that we would have done better.

If Jeremiah's going back on his call highlights the difference
between himself and Jesus, it also obscures the distinction
between the true and the false prophet, which we considered
above. Perhaps the true and the false prophet are in the end
theoretical types: that is, there is not a fixed collection of the
one and a fixed collection of the other. Another reason why
the line between false and true is difficult to draw is that a
false prophet may speak an authentic word, and a true prophet can cease to be the channel of God's message. Perhaps
there is no such thing as a true or a false prophet; there are
only true and false prophecies. If so, then in this lament
Jeremiah makes the transition from one to the other. He turns
back on God's calling and on God's word.

But as a true prophet can fall away, so a false prophet can
return and be restored. He is not necessarily lost, even
though he makes radical mistakes. The stories of Elijah and
Jonah make that clear. But so does this story of Jeremiah's
reaching breaking-point and of the Lord's response to him on
this occasion.

> Therefore Yahweh says,
> If you turn back, I will have you back
> to stand before me.

*If you utter what is valuable instead of what is worthless,
you will be as my own mouth.
They will have to come back to you,
you will not have to go back to them.
I will make you into a fortified wall of bronze before this
     people.
They will fight you, but not overcome you,
for I will be with you to deliver you and to keep you safe.
This is Yahweh's message (15:19-20).*

Jeremiah has got out his prophetic credentials, torn them
up, and trampled them in the mud, like a child angrily
spurning the gift that was not what he wanted. But God
responds like the father who retrieves the spurned gift and
puts it together again to show the child how it works and
how it could be worth having after all. God in turn takes up
the themes of Jeremiah's call and reaffirms them. 'I am with
you to keep you safe'? Yes, *I am with you to deliver you and
to keep you safe.* 'I have put my words in your mouth'? Yes,
you will be as my own mouth. 'I am making you a fortified
city, an iron pillar, and bronze walls against Judah; they will
fight but not prevail over you'? Yes, that is all still true
(15:20, compare 1:18-19).

But there is a condition attached. *If you turn back ... If you
utter what is valuable instead of what is worthless.* The arms
of love remain open; the commissioning hand remains raised.
The call can always be renewed. God promises that there can
still be forgiveness, usefulness, and success (15:19), that there
can still be strength and protection (15:20). *If you turn back.*
If your mouth (which in the previous verses has been used for
Jeremiah's own words) becomes a vehicle for God's words
again.

I have suggested previously that through his life I imagine
Jeremiah lived with a tension between outward certainty and
inner conflict. He lived also, I suspect, with another tension,
which was, indeed, part of his inner conflict, a tension
between the experience of chapter 1 and the experience of
chapter 15. The flesh ever called him to the outburst of
chapter 15, but the spirit drew him back to the call from
which he could not finally escape. It was a real tension. But

the last word should be with the gracious, persisting, calling God. 'I acknowledged you. I set you apart. I appointed you. You are to go to anyone to whom I send you, and to say anything that I tell you. I will be with you to keep you safe. I have put my words in your mouth.' And 'if you turn back, I will have you back to stand before me. If you utter what is valuable instead of what is worthless, you will be as my own mouth.'

CHAPTER FIVE

The moment of fulfilment

The book of Jeremiah ends in a slightly puzzling way, with the unpleasant story of the last days of the reign of King Zedekiah. It is not only an unpleasant story, but also potentially a boring one if the reader knows the preceding books of the Old Testament, because it has already been told at the end of the books of Kings (2 Kings 25), at the end of the books of Chronicles (2 Chr. 36), and even earlier on in the book of Jeremiah (Jer. 39). If there is any chapter that could happily have been left out of the Bible, surely this is it? Why was it included?

The story recounts how Zedekiah rebelled against Nebuchadrezzar, as his brother Jehoiakim had done a decade previously. The Babylonian king came to put down the rebellion, and laid siege to Jerusalem (52:3-5). Old Testament Jerusalem had a strong position. Not only was it on the ridge of a mountain range, but it was on a spur of this range, with the ground falling away sharply on three sides. It was thus difficult to capture from the east or the south or the west: an attacking army is climbing up a steep hill and the people at the top are dropping boulders on its heads. It is not this fact alone, however, that explains how Jerusalem could survive an eighteen-month siege. Half way through, the book of Jeremiah tells us earlier on, the Egyptians came to help Judah, as Zedekiah hoped, and Nebuchadrezzar had to go off to settle them (see Jer. 37). This no doubt gave the people chance to replenish their supplies.

But in due course Nebuchadrezzar returned, shortage of food became very severe in the city, and eventually there was no bread left at all (52:6). This unemotive phrase clearly describes a grim situation, which should perhaps remind us of those pictures of refugees dying in the gutter in Tchad and of babies in Ethiopia who are just skin and bone. Indeed, it was in a way worse than this, as we learn from the poems in the book of Lamentations (five psalms belonging to the period of the exile). The level of human degradation was such that women were reduced to eating the flesh of their own children (see Lam. 2:20). It had happened before in a siege of Samaria (2 Kings 6:24-29). Perhaps people found themselves asking whether Nebuchadrezzar could do worse to them by capturing them than he had done by besieging them. Finally the gates were opened (52:7) and Nebuchadrezzar rode in.

Knowing that they were in the greatest danger, no doubt, Zedekiah and his soldiers took to flight, managing to find their way through the Babylonian lines down into the Arabah, the desert region that starts immediately east of Jerusalem and extends down the mountains to the oasis of Jericho and the Dead Sea. It is an area that the Jews have often taken refuge in; perhaps Zedekiah reckoned that now for a time they would have to become a guerrilla army, until the Babylonians tired of searching for them in the desert. But the Babylonians found Zedekiah and marched him to Nebuchadrezzar's headquarters in Syria. From there he was taken in humiliation to Babylon as another living proof of Nebuchadrezzar's might. But as a punishment for his disloyalty, and to make sure that no-one ever contemplated putting him on a throne again—what use is a blind man as a king?—his sight was destroyed. Probably they did it by searing his eyes with red-hot iron. The final image that he took with him to Babylon was his own sons' death. Zedekiah, the youngest son of Josiah, was a man of about 40. His sons will have been little boys or teenagers. But they were potential successors to

his throne. So the last thing that his eyes beheld was the death
of these boys. *The king of Babylon slew Zedekiah's sons
before his eyes. He also slew all the nobles of Judah at Riblah.
He blinded Zedekiah's eyes and bound him in chains. Thus
the king of Babylon took him to Babylon and put him in
prison until he died* (52:10-11).

The remainder of this closing chapter of Jeremiah describes
the sack of Jerusalem itself. The temple, the palace, and the
housing generally were set on fire, and the walls of Jerusalem
were demolished. The fitments and vessels of the temple
(which are described in poignant detail) were appropriated.
The chief priest and some other temple officials, as well as
some military and political figures, were killed. Anyone else
of any significance was taken off to Babylon. There is a tiny
note of hope in the final paragraph, which relates how the
already-exiled King Jehoiachin was released from prison by
Nebuchadrezzar's son, Evilmerodach. But apart from that, it
is a grim story.

So why is it in the Bible? One reason may be that it reflects
the Bible's recognition of the tragic side to human existence. It
acknowledges that human life is characterized by disaster and
death, by calamity and grief, by misfortune and loss. Zedekiah
was one of the younger of Josiah's sons. He was never destined to be king, and he was not actually equipped for it. But
circumstances took him to the throne. On the throne of
Judah, he was not so much a really wicked king as a rather
feeble one. The stories in the book of Jeremiah that involve
him (see Jer. 32-35; 37-39) suggest that he wanted to follow
the counsel of Jeremiah, recognizing it as both religious truth
and political sense. But he lacked the moral strength to resist
the heady courage of the generals urging him to go for
independence and to throw off Babylonian rule. Consequently
he was unable to avert calamity from Judah, and indeed
brought calamity on his own family and on himself.

This is the tragedy of Zedekiah, and it exemplifies the
tragedy that often seems to characterize human life. We see
people making misguided choices, decisions which clearly
threaten calamity but which seem impossible to avert. We see
it in the Middle East still, or in Northern Ireland. But we see
it also nearer home in our own national life, where we seem

bent on bringing disaster on ourselves and unable to see what makes sense morally or even pragmatically.

Now of course we do not need the Bible to tell us about these things; we know them too well without it. But we may note nevertheless that the Bible does describe this kind of world. Christianity is not a religion that hides from the realities of life; it faces up to them. Sometimes Christians have hidden from these realities, or behaved as if life in its tragedy and calamity were nothing to do with God, who is concerned only with prayer and church. But the world is God's world, and the Bible recognizes that there is about human life this element of the tragic; and it says that God is involved in it.

Thus the story of the fall of Jerusalem presupposes that history is in the control of the God of Israel. Even in this tragedy, with its human mistakes and its sin and evil, his purpose is being worked out. *Jerusalem and Judah so angered the LORD that in the end he banished them from his sight; and Zedekiah rebelled against the king of Babylon* (52:3 NEB). It is striking how the two parts of that sentence fit together. God decided that enough was enough; the time for him to act had come. His anger had to receive expression. But what happens is not that God sends an earthquake to destroy Jerusalem, or that a flash of lightning from heaven consumes it. *Zedekiah rebelled against the king of Babylon;* and Zedekiah knew what he was doing. He made his decision and he put it into effect. Yet at the same time it was the working out of God's will. Nebuchadrezzar knew what he was doing. He did it for good political reasons. Yet unknown to him, he was Yahweh's servant, Jeremiah says (Jer. 25:9); it was Yahweh who brought him up against the Jews, say the books of Chronicles (2 Chron. 36:17). Men's own free decisions are the means by which God works out his purpose. It is thus he who controls history. He proves this by frustrating man's purpose when he needs to. After the fall of the city Zedekiah fled towards the Arabah, and there his troops scattered (Jer. 52:7-8). Yet even in that wilderness the Babylonians found him. How did that come about? Well, after all, 'they had God, as it were, as their guide', comments Calvin (*Commentary on the Book of Jeremiah*, Volume IV, 1950, p.426). Nebuchadrezzar put an end

to the rule of the Davidic line in Jerusalem, burned down the
temple, took its vessels to Babylon, broke down the city's
walls, and deported its remaining worthwhile citizens to
Babylon; but within 150 years there have been Davidic
princes back in Jerusalem, the temple is rebuilt and function-
ing again, as many of the people as wish to return are back,
the city walls are rebuilt, and it is the Babylonian empire that
is now only a figure in the history books. And this further
reversal comes about because history is in the control of the
God of Israel.

It is perhaps surprising, however, that this same history so
often seems to bring trouble on Israel herself, and thus dis-
credit on Yahweh's name. But this fact draws attention to
another implication of the presence in the Bible of a story
such as this one. It is that God has a *righteous* purpose to
fulfil in history. *Jerusalem and Judah angered the LORD*
(52:3). It is not that he is rather fickle and loses his temper
inexplicably. It is that they *did what was wrong in the eyes of
the LORD* (52:2 NEB). They ignored the Torah and the
messages of prophets such as Jeremiah. They ignored Yahweh's standards of justice, morality, and mercy. They either
placed a false trust in him, as if he were unconditionally
committed to them for ever, or they turned their backs on
him and worshipped other gods.

The Old Testament (particularly Ezekiel) pictures God
placed in a certain dilemma by this eventuality. He has taken
the risk of committing himself to this people and to their
king. His reputation and his purpose are tied up with them. If
he abandons them, he punishes himself. If he lets them off, he
frustrates his own moral purpose. Neither a sinful people, nor
a destroyed people, could reveal to the world a holy and
loving God. On the one hand, he does banish them from his
sight (52:3). But precisely because his purpose is to reveal
himself to the world, this cannot be his last word. Indeed,
Jeremiah has already told us that beyond judgement there
will be restoration. He has made his surprising investment in
real estate when the siege of Jerusalem was temporarily alle-
viated, though its eventual fall remained inevitable (see Jer.
32-33). That was a concrete expression of Jeremiah's commitment to the certainty that a time would come when land

would be bought and sold again in the country that Nebucha-drezzar was bent on devastating. In the same context, Jeremiah speaks of the renewing of the broken covenant between Yahweh and Israel, of its renewing on a better and more permanent basis than before (Jer.31:31-34; 32:36-41).

Again, the last chapter of Jeremiah speaks of the evil deeds of King Zedekiah and of his humiliation and disfiguring by Nebuchadrezzar (Jer.52:2-3, 9-11). But Zedekiah is a prince of the line of David, that line to which God made his eternal commitment, and of which the Messiah was to be born. Here, Calvin again comments, 'Lying prostrate at the feet of a proud conqueror' is 'a king ... who was a type of Christ' (*Commentary ...*, Volume IV, p.428). This humiliation cannot be God's last word. Indeed, as with the new covenant, Jeremiah has already told us it is not. Zedekiah's own name means 'Yahweh is my *righteousness*, my vindication.' God has already promised that he is going to raise up for David's fallen tree a *righteous* branch, who will execute *righteousness* in the land, and who will be called 'Yahweh-zidkenu' (23:5-6). The king is called 'Yahweh is my righteousness'; but he does not live up to the name and must be cast off. But one day there will be a king worthy of the name, 'Yahweh is our righteousness'. The same *righteous* purpose of God that brings the fall of Jerusalem and the exile of Zedekiah, also guarantees the fulfilment of God's purpose of restoration in the future. Destruction is not God's *last* word to his people.

This leads us to a further insight as to why this story appears in the Bible, and more specifically as to why it comes in this particular place, at the end of the book of Jeremiah (and not merely in the historical books). Why are we not told about the rest of Jeremiah's life? Why is it left to legends to tell us how he died?

Perhaps the answer lies in the fact that the book of Jeremiah is not essentially about Jeremiah. It is about the word of God. The book itself begins the way other prophetic books do: *These are the words of Jeremiah ... Yahweh's word came to him ...* (Jer. 1:1-2). It is a book about words. Even the stories are about what happens to God's *word.* They are accounts of how people respond to God's word, not merely to Jeremiah. If it is right to look at the book as a whole in this way, then

the final chapter may after all be a very appropriate end to it.
The chapter tells, in a quite matter-of-fact way, of how events
turned out just as God had said. The word of his prophet is
proved right. Even though Jeremiah himself is not mentioned
in this final chapter, it is the vindication of *his* ministry.

It thus also suggests that the other side of his word will be
fulfilled. Jeremiah's message was, 'Yahweh will break this
covenant and make a new one; he will depose this king and
bring forth a new branch from the stump of Jesse.' If the first
half of the declaration is fulfilled, the latter will be too.

But what is the proof of this? *The word of our God endures
forever* (Isa. 40:8). That statement of faith takes us from the
book of Jeremiah to the book of Isaiah. Although we can
listen to people's numbed response to the fall of Jerusalem
and to the exile in Lamentations and in Psalm 137, the prophecies of Isaiah of the exile reflect that response also.

> *The path I tread is hidden from Yahweh,*
> *my cause has passed out of God's notice (40:27).*
>
> *Yahweh has abandoned me.*
> *The Lord has forgotten me (49:14).*
>
> *These two things have happened to you—*
> *who is there to grieve with you?*
> *Devastation and destruction, famine and sword—*
> *how can I comfort you? (51:19).*
>
> *All mankind is grass,*
> *they last as long as a wild flower.*
> *Grass withers, flowers fade,*
> *when Yahweh's breath blows on them.*
> *Certainly the people are grass (40:6-7).*

The prophet himself shares these feelings as an Israelite in
exile. But he describes them as the background for the word
from God that he declares, which brings good news to people
who believe that they have no comforter because they have
been abandoned and forgotten by God. 'Yes, you have been
under God's judgement', he says, 'But that's over now.
Yahweh had turned his face away from you, but now he has
come back.'

> *Comfort, comfort my people, says your God*
> *Encourage Jerusalem, proclaim to her:*
> *Her bondage is over, her penalty is paid;*
> *She has received from Yahweh's hand*
> *full punishment for her sins (40:1-2).*

The prophet is commissioned to preach to a people whose faith is burnt out, whose morale is gone, whose hope is extinguished, and to tell such a people that their God is alive, he does care, and he is about to return to them. They said, *The path I tread is hidden from Yahweh, my cause has passed out of God's notice.* He replied, *Do you not know? Have you not heard? Yahweh is the eternal God ... He gives strength to the weary ...* (40:27-31). They said, *The Lord has forgotten me.* He declared, *Can a woman forget the baby she feeds ...? Even if these should forget, I will not forget you* (49:14-15). They said there was no-one to comfort them in their distress (51:19). He declared, *Comfort my people* (40:1). They said they felt like grass scorched by the sun. He replied, Yes, *the grass withers, the flowers fade; but the word of our God* (the commitment he has made to his people, his promises to them) *endures for ever* (40:6-8). This is the message of Isaiah in the exile. He is concerned to meet God's people where they are, to lift their spirits, to build up their faith, to re-establish their morale, to restore their hope, to rebuild their commitment. His message is that God has not cast them off, he has not finished with them. The moment has come when he will restore them. *The mouth of Yahweh has spoken* (40:5).

Isaiah 40-55

'He said to me ... "I shall appoint you as a light
to the nations" '
(Isaiah 49:3,6)

CHAPTER SIX

The chosen servant (Isaiah 41:1-20)

So the Isaiah of the exile is called to bring a message of comfort and challenge to Jews who have been in exile for a half a century—most of whom, therefore, have never known anything else. As he brings this message, one of his recurrent themes is the motif of the servant of Yahweh, an idea that appears in most of the chapters (see, for instance, 41:8-10; 42:1,19; 43:10; 44:1,21; 45:4; 48:20; 49:3-6; 50:10; 52:13; 53:11; 54:17). It is a key motif which expresses some of the most important aspects of his message.

If asked whom Isaiah meant in his prophecies when he spoke of the servant of the Lord, most Christians would reply that he was talking about Jesus Christ, and this is certainly the major thrust of the New Testament's references to passages from Isaiah about the servant. Even in the New Testament, however, the possibility of other views is recognized. The question is raised by the Ethiopian official who was reading the most detailed of the passages about the servant (Isa. 53) when he was met by Philip the evangelist (see Acts 8:26-40). Puzzled by what he is reading, the Ethiopian's first thought is that the prophet is speaking of himself. When we go back to Isaiah 40-55 itself, however, we find that the chapters' first

reference to the servant explicitly identifies the servant as
Israel (Isa. 41:8-10).

These three possibilities—that the servant is Jesus, that it is
the prophet himself, that it is Israel—all have their supporters
today. In my view, there is truth in all of them. The servant
calling belongs first to Israel as the people of God. She cannot
fulfil it, however, and God calls the prophet himself to be his
servant. But the prophet realizes that in its ultimate dimensions the role of the servant embodies a vision which goes
beyond his calling. The Christian finds it fulfilled in Jesus, but
also sees it as passed on by him to those who follow him and
those who claim to represent him.

But this is to anticipate a picture which develops only as
the chapters unfold. We must begin with Israel.

REASONS FOR DISMAY

But you are Israel my servant,
Jacob whom I chose,
the descendants of Abraham my friend.
I took you from the ends of the earth,
I called you from its farthest corners.
I said to you 'You are my servant',
I chose you, I did not reject you.
Do not look about in fear,
I am with you, I am your God.
I strengthen you, I help you,
I support you with my right hand; it sees to what is right
(41:8-10).

The heart of the opening message about the servant lies here.
'Don't be afraid, Israel. You are my chosen servant. I am
alongside you.'

These verses themselves, and their context, suggest several
reasons why the Israelites in exile might have been afraid.
They would have been naturally fearful about world affairs.
They were living at a time of international unrest, a time
when the Persian king, Cyrus was beginning to rampage
around the Middle East. He is trampling kings under foot,
making them like dust with his sword, advancing from city to

city so fast his feet seem scarcely to touch the ground (41:2-3). It is a time of world uncertainty, when no-one can be quite sure what will happen next, like living in Eastern Europe in 1939 or 1944, or like living in the Middle East today. The prophet describes how the people of Babylon itself were responding to this situation:

> The coastlands have seen this, and are afraid.
> The ends of the earth tremble with fear.
> They have come and assembled.
> Each man helps his neighbour
> and says to his mate, 'Take courage!'
> The craftsman encourages the goldsmith,
> the man who beats out the metal with the hammer
>   encourages the one who strikes the nails,
> saying of the solder, 'That's good',
> and fastening it with nails so that it will not move (41:5-7).

It is a pathetic picture of desperate attempts to cope when history seems to be collapsing. People are naturally afraid and dismayed because of world affairs. They naturally respond by manufacturing their own solutions.

What is Isaiah's response? What is the word of Yahweh in such a situation? It is striking that the prophet does not speak as though this historical crisis is outside God's purpose. One might not have been surprised if the purported word of Yahweh had asserted, 'Yes, the tyrant Cyrus, Yahweh's enemy, is advancing and will cause terrible trouble, but you must stand firm and believe that God will protect his people.' This was in fact approximately what the Babylonian priests would say about their God. The prophet of Yahweh does not say that world affairs are going the opposite way to what God wants, but that he will nevertheless deliver you. Rather, like Jeremiah, he declares that world events are working out in exactly the way Yahweh wants. It is for this reason that his people have no reason to fear. God is not just someone to protect them from crises; he is someone who brings about crises. He is the Lord of history.

The prophet makes this point by challenging people in general to give some explanation of where Cyrus came from. Often in these chapters, he is nominally addressing the whole

world. But in reality, it is Israel herself he is trying to
encourage to think.

> Keep silence before me, you coastlands.
> Let the peoples summon up new strength,
> let them come forward and speak.
> Let us meet together to give judgement.
> Who roused one from the east,
> one whom a righteous purpose greets at every step?
> He gives nations over to him,
> he subdues kings,
> His sword makes them like dust,
> his bow makes them like straw blowing in the wind.
> He pursues them and passes on from success to success,
> his feet do not touch the road.
> Who acted, who did it,
> summoning the course of history from the beginning?
> I, Yahweh, I am the first,
> and I am with the last. I am the one (41:1-4).

It is Yahweh, the God of Israel, who is bringing about this historical crisis. It is therefore entirely natural for the Babylonians
to panic (41:5). But it is not natural for Israel to do so, because
the same God who is the Lord of historical crises is the God
who promises to look after Israel. The historical crises are
part of his gracious will. His people can relax when the world
seems to be falling apart, because they know who is making it
fall apart; they know who is in control. The Babylonians
tremble; *but you are Israel my servant, Jacob whom I chose
... Do not look about in fear, I am with you* (41:8,10). The
Babylonians are in a panic because of somebody coming from
the east, but you are the children of one who came from the
east, *you are ... the descendants of Abraham my friend. I
took you from the ends of the earth, I called you from its
farthest corners. I said to you 'You are my servant', I chose
you, I did not reject you* (41:8-9). The Babylonians are
dismayed at the victories of Cyrus: but your God gives him
those victories, they are the righteous achievements of his
right hand, active on your behalf (41:10). The Babylonians
desperately look to each other for help and strength like
drunks hoping to find support by leaning on each other: but

the Lord strengthens you, the Lord upholds you (41:10). The
people of God have no reason to be fearful or dismayed
about world affairs, because the Lord of world affairs is their
Lord and they are his servants.

The exiles would also feel a natural fear of the people they
had to live among. It was the usual Jewish story; they formed
an alien element in a hostile environment. They did not really
belong in the country they lived in; indeed, at this point in
time, they had not at all chosen to go to this particular place.
They had been taken there by force as prisoners of war and
dumped in a refugee camp, like Arab refugees in the Middle
East today. They were not popular with the people they had
to live among. Physically, in actual fact, they were reasonably
well off. They had their own communities, places of meeting
and leadership. Indeed they were sufficiently comfortable for
many to prefer to stay there when the chance to go home
came. But nevertheless they formed an alien element in a
hostile environment, and it would be natural to be afraid of
those they had to live among.

But it is these opponents who are in a state of panic over
the advance of Cyrus, it is these who have no way of coping
with the way world affairs are unfolding. So here is the word
of the Lord in relation to *that* need.

*All those who rage at you will know disappointment and
shame.*
Those who quarrel with you will vanish into nothing.
*You will look for those who attack you, but not be able to
find them.*
*Those who do battle with you will cease to exist at all
(41:11-12).*

In these two verses the hostility of their enemies is described
in sharper and sharper terms. First it is annoyance (11a), then
opposition (11b), then attack (12a), finally war (12b). This is
not just vivid imagination. The Babylonians have actually
behaved in such ways in relation to Israel in the years that led
up to the exile. The prophet assumes (as no doubt the exiles
assume) that the Babylonians are not going to change character overnight as Cyrus advances; perhaps rather the opposite.

He is quite realistic about the peril the Jews are in. He does not underestimate the danger that comes from those they live among. He can face it openly, because he has the answer: he knows that God is going to deal with it. He knows that the sharper is their opposition, the more complete is their downfall. Thus, at the same time as his description of their enemies' hostility gets sharper and sharper, his promise of how they will be dealt with gets more and more devastating. First they will be put to shame (11a), then they will disappear (11b), then you will not be able to find them (12a), finally they cease to exist at all (12b).

We ought perhaps to recall whom the prophet is speaking of. It is the mighty Babylonian empire, the people who built the ziggurats and the hanging gardens of Babylon, the people who had twice besieged and conquered Jerusalem, and who now held the leading Israelites in exile. Of them he says, 'Do not assume they are going to get more friendly: the coming crisis is likely to have the opposite effect. Nevertheless, even as their hostility increases, you will see them put to shame, vanish, disappear, cease to exist. The bigger they are, the harder they fall.'

The prophet knows this, because he knows who Israel's God is. *For I, Yahweh, your God, I hold you by the hand* (41:13). Remember who Yahweh is? He is the creator of the ends of the earth (40:28: see 40:12-31 generally). He is the Lord of history from beginning to end who is also active in present world affairs (41:4). This is *the one who says to you, 'Do not be afraid, I will help you'* (41:13). Again we recall the prophet's description of the threatened Babylonians desperately trying to prop each other up as the crisis-point draws near (41:5-7), and we hear Yahweh saying to his people, 'Do not be afraid of those around you. *I* will be *your* help'.

Further, the exiles would naturally be dismayed at the obstacles that lay between them and their return to their own land. This seems to be the point of the reference to the Israelites being confronted by mountains and hills (41:14-16). The prophet has spoken earlier of mountains and hills: *every valley will rise up, and every mountain and hill lie flat* (40:4). There he was certainly alluding to the obstacles that hindered Yahweh's return to Jerusalem. Those obstacles would be removed, the prophet declared. As a motorway carves its way across a landscape, scything its path through the hills and supported by embankments over the valleys, so Yahweh's highway will take him back to Jerusalem. And his people will travel with him (40:10-11). Their exile is coming to an end. He is going home; and they are going home too.

But the obstacles to the people getting home were huge, indeed mountain-sized. The opposition of the Babylonians, which we have already referred to, is one such obstacle. Another is the sheer distance and the physical obstacles in the way. It is not primarily mountain-country but desert, yet nevertheless a huge obstacle separating Babylon from Jerusalem. Another obstacle would be the sheer perversity of the exiles themselves; when the gospels speak of mountains and valleys being levelled before the Lord comes (see especially Luke 3:1-14), it is moral obstacles to God's working that they have in mind. Huge barriers seemed to hinder the people's getting back home; mountains and hills dismayed them. That was the worm's eye-view: Israel felt exactly like a tiny worm before them (41:14).

The prophet would grant that a worm can make little impression on a mountain. But God promises that he intends to turn Israel from a worm into a threshing sledge (41:15). A threshing sledge was a wooden platform with bits of iron or stone set in the bottom. After the corn had been cut and collected together for threshing, the farmer sat or stood on his threshing sledge while his oxen pulled it back and forward, round and round, over the corn, till it was all cut up into tiny bits. Then he could fork it into the air so that the wind would carry the chaff away. Now, says Yahweh,

> I am making you into a threshing-sledge,
> a new one, studded with teeth.
> You will be able to thresh the mountains and crush them,
> and make the hills like chaff.
> You will be able to winnow them so that the wind can take
> them and the storm scatter them (41:15-16).

The obstacles to Israel going home look like mountains. But Israel will overcome them as easily as the farmer crushes the grain and disposes of the chaff. No matter how huge are the obstacles that stand between the place where God's people are and the place of God's blessing where he purposes to take them, these obstacles cannot withstand God's plan to fulfil his promises to them.

What are the grounds for the prophet's conviction of this? How can he get people to believe him? *I am the one who helps you*, says Yahweh once again. *Your redeemer is the holy one of Israel* (41:14). Those two descriptions of God are very important; it is in them that the justification for Isaiah's confidence lies. He speaks in the name of 'the holy one of Israel'. This theme, as we have noted above, runs through the whole book of Isaiah. It goes back to Isaiah's vision of God exalted in glory (Isaiah 6). There the seraphim acknowledged him as the ultimate holy one: *'Holy, holy, holy is Almighty Yahweh'* (6:3). Overhearing their worship, Isaiah of Jerusalem took this as a keynote of his message. Israel's God is the holy one. But Israel had failed him, indeed had rebelled against him. Therefore because he is the holy one, he will punish her. That is Isaiah's message in the eighth century.

With the exile the punishment came. The holy one had proved that he was holy by his act of judgement. Now the message is to be different. Yahweh is still the holy one of Israel. He is still attached to Israel. He is still faithful to his own commitment to her. The fact that he was the holy one of Israel was a threat to her when she was in a state of sin. But now in her state of need it is a comfort to her.

This point is made explicit by declaring that this holy one is Israel's *redeemer*. Here is another word with a long history. It means a close relative, someone who belongs to your fairly immediate family. Such a person had obligations to you: if you were in need, he had to help you. For instance, if you got into debt and had to sell your land, or even to sell yourself into slavery to pay the debt, your close relatives were under moral obligation to come to your aid. The two nearest English words are 'next-of-kin' and 'guardian'—the word, that is, suggests a member of your family who steps in to look after your interests when you cannot look after yourself.

So, the prophet says, you can be sure that Yahweh will fulfil his word to you and that the huge obstacles that cut you

off from your homeland can be overcome, because the holy
one of Israel is your next-of-kin, your guardian. You belong
to the same family as he does, and he is the close relative who
steps in to look after your interests in this situation where you
cannot look after yourself. So again, you have no reason to
look about in fear.

Yet another reason for the exiles to feel dismay is expressed
in a further paragraph (41:17-20). It reveals a further aspect
of how Israel feels: poor and needy, seeking water but finding
none, parched with thirst. Again, the picture takes up an
aspect of life in Palestine. In Britain, sun is good news, rain is
bad news. In May or June as summer approaches our spirits
are raised, in October or November as winter draws near
they probably flag. In Palestine it is the other way round. In
summer the sun bakes the land dry and kills nearly everything that grows, as it did in Britain for once in a century in
1976. People look forward to October or November and to
the rain, because it means the revival of nature. If the rains
fail, nature stays lifeless. The crops fail. The animals die of
thirst.

That experience of baking drought every summer (and of
drought at other times, if people were unfortunate) suggests a
way people in the Bible, particularly in the Psalms, describe
themselves when they are in need. We are like the land parched for lack of rain. As Ezekiel puts it in his vision of the
valley of dry bones, 'Our bones are dried up, our hope has
gone; we are as good as dead' (Ezek. 37:11 JB). We have been
abandoned. We have nowhere to find refreshment or renewal.

Here is Isaiah's response to that lament.

> The poor and needy are looking for water, and there is
>   none;
> their tongues are parched with thirst.
> I, Yahweh, will answer them;
> as the God of Israel I will not abandon them (41:17).

'You think it is all over, but you are wrong. You have abandoned belief in Yahweh, the God of Israel. You doubt whether
it is worth pleading with him about the situation any more.
So you feel like the Judaean wilderness, those bare sun-baked

slopes where a man can lose himself and die of heat and thirst within a few miles of civilization. But imagine those bare hills suddenly irrigated, watered, planted, forested. I could do that for your lives.'

> *I can open up rivers in land that is bare*
> *and fountains in the middle of valleys.*
> *I can make the wilderness into a lake*
> *and arid land into springs of water.*
> *In the wilderness I can place cedar trees,*
> *acacias, myrtles, olive trees.*
> *In the desert I can put junipers,*
> *pines and cypresses side by side (41:18-19).*

The feeling that you are cut off from all sources of renewal, that everything has run dry, is not reason for dismay, for the Lord remains able to open up springs in the desert. He can bring refreshment to places that are dry and parched.

THE UNDERLYING FEAR

There, then, are the pressures which drive Israel to the ground: the world affairs that threaten her; the attitude of people around her; the obstacles that confront her; the personal needs within her. But there is one other cause of dismay which lies just under the surface of these feelings. We have come close to it in passing just now, for we have noted that God says, *I will not abandon them* (41:17). That promise hints at a further and most fundamental reason for the exiles' dismay. They were afraid that, whereas they used to be able to turn to Yahweh when world events threatened them or people attacked them or obstacles confronted them or personal needs depressed them, now they can do that no longer. Yahweh himself has abandoned them. The fall of Jerusalem and the dragging years in exile make that quite clear. He has finished with them. This is why fear, referred to three times in five verses (41:10,13,14), has replaced faith. They are afraid, not merely of the Persians or the Babylonians. They are afraid of the future, afraid of life itself without Yahweh, afraid of

Yahweh himself, who they know still exists (people in the ancient world never seemed to doubt the *existence* of their gods) but who now seems to be permanently against them instead of being for them.

There is another hint of this feeling in the paragraph about drought and refreshment (41:17-20). Sometimes one of our children would come to my wife or me and say, 'Will you read me a book?' or 'Will you take us swimming?' or 'Can I have a biscuit?' At other times (perhaps because we had already said no) they would mooch around in a dejected way talking under their breath to no-one in particular. 'I wish there was someone to read me a book.' 'I wish we could go swimming.' 'I'm starving.' There is an important difference between those two ways of speaking. One is a request addressed to a person who could actually meet it; and there is evidently reckoned to be a fair chance that he or she will. The other presupposes (rightly or wrongly) that he or she is not interested or is bound to say no, and it is really a lament at the unsatisfactoriness of life rather than an actual request.

Adults in their own way lament the unsatisfactoriness of life, too; no doubt we learned to do it when we were children. We bemoan whatever is getting on top of us, bemoan it to ourselves; we can talk only to ourselves about it, because there is no-one else to tell about it, is there?

Apparently what Israel was doing was not so very different from this. The poor and needy are seeking water and finding none and their tongue is parched with thirst... It is all very indirect, like the children mooching round the living room resentful of some deprivation but knowing it is no use trying to interest the parents in it. Israel is not really praying, she is just complaining out loud, because she no longer believes God is interested. God responds, nevertheless: *I will answer them.* Israel's deepest need is for a reassurance of God's concern about her. Her morale has sunk back to the point it reached in her time in Egypt (see Exod. 2:23-24). There *the Israelites groaned under their bondage, and cried out.* There, too, it was no prayer; they lacked the resources any longer to lift their eyes Godwards. They could only lament their affliction. But nevertheless *their cry under bondage came up to God. God heard their groaning...* God was still bending his ear downwards. He took note of their distress and acted. The biggest challenge for Isaiah in the exile, too, is to convince Israel that God is still listening and still cares.

Now it is in this connection that he reminds them that Israel is Yahweh's servant. *I said to you, 'You are my servant.' I chose you, I did not reject you* (41:9). The fear that Yahweh has forsaken them underlies all their other fears. So the assurance that he has not abandoned them, and will not, underlies all the prophet's other promises.

'You are my chosen servant.' The idea of being God's servant makes its first appearance in these prophecies as a re-assurance for Israel as to her status with God. He is committed to her. He chose her. He gave her a relationship with him. He will not terminate the relationship. 'You are my chosen servant. You have no reason to give up prayer, no reason to give in to fear.'

Fear is one of the most elemental and basic of man's feelings in his fallen state. Adam and Eve hiding in the garden, Cain terrified at being alone in the world, the men who half-built the city of Babel with its tower because they were afraid, Abraham fearful lest the pharaoh kills him because he fancies Sarah: fear is a basic human emotion.

Of course fear should not be seen as essentially sinful. There is a right fear of God which we will keep even in heaven. There is a right fear of danger, of crises, and of challenges, that stops one being foolhardy and encourages one to apply oneself to the task in hand. At another extreme, fear can come to possess a person's whole personality. Healthy apprehension which encourages revision before examinations, becomes a paralysing panic that makes work impossible. A prudent concern about germs becomes an irrational phobia which makes a woman never cease washing her hands. But most of us are not afflicted by that. Yet we do fall into the kinds of anxiety the exiles felt. Humanly speaking, both their fears of world events and of people around, and their dismay at the obstacles that confronted them and at their own personal needs, were entirely rational. Humanly speaking, it was an appropriate response to a fearful set of circumstances.

But these human evaluations are confronted by the 'gospel'. The prophet uses this expression (40:9) in speaking of good news being brought to the exiles: the good news is that God is working out his purpose through world events, that he can deal with people who oppose the exiles, that he can remove the obstacles that separate the people of God from their destiny, that he can bring refreshment to places that are dry and parched.

When the people of God are in a situation where, humanly speaking, fear is the appropriate response, what God does is to give them his promises. That is all, at first. They are left with the situation, and with the word which promises that 'humanly speaking' is not all there is. They are challenged to let fear give way to trust, because of these promises. If they do, then the place of fear can be a place of growth.

Thus fear can be replaced by rejoicing and glorying in the Lord. That is a final point made by this section of Isaiah's collected prophecies. Because he is going to do all this,

You can rejoice in Yahweh,
in the holy one of Israel you can glory (41:16).

The prophet's concern is that the good news of restoration which he brings should not merely be a comfort to Israel, but should also lead to a return movement of praise and worship from Israel to God. This is his final aim, that God may have the glory. If they were to enjoy God's blessings and not give him the glory, then an important aspect of the point of the whole thing would be lost.

It is on this note that the whole section actually ends: not merely with the praise of Israel, but with the praise of the world. When God makes the wilderness of Israel's life into a green oasis, the ultimate aim is

that people may see and acknowledge,
may give heed and understand,
that it is Yahweh's hand which has done this,
it is the holy one of Israel who has created it (41:20).

CHAPTER SEVEN

The faithful servant (Isaiah 41:21-42:17)

So Israel enjoys the privilege, the status, and the position of Yahweh's servant. The prophet goes on to describe what it means to be God's servant and what God's servant is called to. He offers a job-description for the servant of Yahweh. It is the calling Israel was supposed to fulfil.

The job-description is contained in two prophecies which are now combined together (42:1-4,5-9). The first (1-4) describes God's servant, talking about him. The second (5-9) addresses God's servant, talking to him. The actual term 'servant' does not appear in the second passage, but it seems to be referring to the same person as do the previous verses. The two passages are two accounts of how God commissions his servant, one to tell other people, the other to tell him. But they are parallel in content, and similar themes recur.

Both begin with a kind of recap. *Here is my servant ...* (42:1). The prophet describes Yahweh's servant in the same terms he has used earlier. 'You remember the servant we were speaking of before—the one *whom I support* (see 41:10), *the one I chose* (see 41:8), *the one in whom I delight.*' (These last words have not come previously, though the idea of Israel as the one 'on whom God's favour rests' (cf. C.R. North, *The*

Second Isaiah, 1967, p.37) is fundamental to chapter 41.)

There is a similar recap when Yahweh begins to speak directly to the servant (42:6): *I am Yahweh. Remember how I called you* (see 41:9) *with a righteous purpose* (see 41:10). *I took you by the hand* (see 41:9). *I kept you.* (Again, these words have not come before; but they summarize 41:8-20. The fact that 'righteousness' in 42:6 recaps 41:10 is not apparent in the modern English translations. The Hebrew word generally translated 'victorious' in 41:10 is the same as the one translated 'righteous' in 42:6. The idea is that God's righteousness is not something abstract and inactive. It makes him get involved in the world giving victory to the cause of righteousness. So both verses refer to this righteousness of God which is active in the world seeing that justice wins the victory).

So Yahweh begins these two prophecies by recalling the position he has given to his servant. His servant is loved by God, chosen by God, called by God, taken by the hand by God, upheld by God, kept by God. The message of comfort which the exiles needed is reasserted. But at this point in Isaiah 40-55 this is only a resumé of the prophet's previous words. What he has to go on to say is more demanding than those words of comfort. There he spoke of the commitment Yahweh makes to his servant, promising to be faithful to him and not to abandon him. Now Yahweh raises the question of the commitment he expects of his servant. Is his servant going to be faithful to him? Or is his servant going to abandon him?

To be chosen and called by God has as its object not just that one can enjoy basking in the sunshine of God's love. One can do that; but the experience is intended then to give to the people of God new resources and new strength with which to serve him. He is committed to them. Are they committed to him? So in these two paragraphs the prophet sets up a vision of what God's servant is called to be. He unfolds what God's idea was in loving and choosing and calling, in taking and keeping and upholding.

WHAT THE SERVANT IS CALLED TO DO

*I have put my spirit on him, he will bring my judgement to
the nations* (42:1). *I have made you a covenant to the people,
a light to the nations* (42:6). The servant is to be the means
whereby Yahweh brings to mankind in general God's judgement, a covenant relationship, illumination.

These declarations have their background in passages earlier
in Isaiah. Isaiah looks forward (see Isa. 2:2-5) to a day when
nations and peoples will flock to Yahweh to learn of his ways
by hearing his law (as in 42:4). Their strife with one another
will end when he gives judgement in the affairs of the nations
(as in 42:1,3,4: God brings a just judgement, his authoritative
decisions concerning the affairs of the nations). Isaiah closes
that prophecy by encouraging Israel herself, having received
God's laws, to walk in this light (compare 42:6). Subsequently
(see 11:1-10), Isaiah speaks of a new David on whom the
spirit of Yahweh will rest (compare 42:1), so that he will have
the wisdom to exercise judgement (the same word as in 42:1,
3,4 again) in a way that is fair and faithful (compare 42:3).

So the world is seen as in a state of chaos and disarray. The
nations have no assured relationship with God. They are in
the dark as to how their lives should be lived. God wants to
bring the order that his just judgement makes possible (his
judgement is not a negative thing, but the sorting out of rights
and wrongs to make true life possible). He wants to give them
a relationship with him that they can rely on, a covenant
relationship like the one he has with Israel. He wants to give
them the light of his revelation, his teaching.

Indeed, the nations apparently realize that. The *coastlands*
(perhaps the areas on Palestine's Mediterranean coastline,
perhaps countries the other side of the Mediterranean—but
they stand here for the gentiles in general) *are waiting for his
teaching,* for the message which the servant will bring them
(42:4). The servant brings Torah (usually translated 'law'):
the statement makes it clear that God's law is not intended to
be something burdensome, and the Old Testament does not
see it as such. Torah means much more than a collection of
laws. It covers teaching in general. God's law is God's revelation, God's word. Thus those who know God's law love it,

rejoice in it, and enthuse over it (as Psalms 19 and 119 show); and those who do not know it are looking forward to discovering it.

They may not be doing so consciously, of course. In order to make life liveable, people often have to hide from facing up to what they lack. They evade the admission that they have so little clue as to what life means, where the world is going, and what their own existence is about. But the prophet presupposes that they are waiting (subconsciously, if not consciously) for someone to tell them the answers to these questions.

The servant's job is to make that possible. He brings God's judgement, God's covenant, God's light. Precisely how he does that is not here explained, though an earlier passage we referred to (Isa. 2) offers some suggestions. One way that Israel will bring light to the world is by letting God's light flood through her own life. Isaiah had urged his hearers, 'Let us walk in Yahweh's light' (2:5). She makes it clear that people can have a covenant relationship with God, by enjoying that relationship herself. This is how the original promise to Abraham was to work. God would bless Abraham in a spectacular way to show what he could do for a man (see Gen. 12:1-3). If Israel lets God's light fill her life, this will make her a beacon which attracts the nations to her. It is then that the nations will flock to Jerusalem, knowing that this is where God's truth can be learned and God's judgement obtained. If men want matters sorted out, they will come to the God of Israel. God's people are expected thus to attract others to him. The point is expressed beautifully a few years later by Zechariah: 'Ten foreigners will come to one Jew and say, "We want to share in your destiny, because we have heard that God is with you" ' (Zech. 8:23 GNB).

The servant brings Yahweh's light to the nations by attracting them to him. He does not seem to be pictured as going out to tell the world about Yahweh. After all, the sun does not bring light to the earth by coming to the earth, but by staying where it is and shining. It is striking how little reference there is in the Old Testament to anything that one might call 'missionary activity'. It is not that the Old Testament assumes that Yahweh the God of Israel is not the God of the whole world or is not interested in the whole world. It is rather that it believes that the way the world is to be won is not by hard-sell proselytizing but by attracting people. Israel is to show in her life what God can do with a people, and thereby to invite them to seek him. Ultimately, indeed, it is not Israel who has to do this. It is God who does it through her. She has only to be available.

If the church now reckons to take on the role of God's means of reaching his world, then she has to accept this insight of Isaiah's. It is particularly relevant when one considers the church's relationship with Israel herself. Christians would love to see Jews recognize that Jesus is their Messiah. But the Christian church in its relationship with Judaism over the centuries has not manifested the light of God in its life. There is such a backlog of darkness in us that it is impossible for us to claim stridently that we have the truth. Jews may reasonably refuse to believe that the Messiah has come when they do not find a messianic people, cannot see the Messiah reigning in justice, and cannot perceive God's judgement, God's covenant grace, or God's light in those who claim to stand for it.

It would be a mistake to swing from one extreme to another and suggest that *all* we have to do is sit here and let people be drawn to us. Jesus did commission his people to go out into the world, and it was in connection with this active task that Paul picks up the motif of the servant bringing light to the world (Acts 13:47). But nevertheless the servant people of God is called to accept the challenge to let the light of God's revelation shine in her own life.

HOW THE SERVANT IS CALLED TO ACT

How is the servant to go about his task?

He will not snap a broken reed,
he will not snuff out a flickering flame (42:3).

Here are two ways of talking about violent death: it is like a reed being snapped, or like a flame being put out (this metaphor re-appears in 43:17). We are to imagine people who are alive, but afflicted and oppressed, and we are to imagine a reed that is not actually snapped off, but is bent and bruised, or a candle that is not actually out, but is very low. People do not try to mend broken reeds; if a reed bends in someone's way, it gets trampled on. People do not take the flickering stub of a candle to read by; they snuff it out and light a new one. That is how the world treats people, too. But Yahweh's servant does not snap off broken reeds; he binds them up and supports them. He does not quench flickering flames; he fans them to a blaze again.

> He'll never quench the smoking flax,
>   But raise it to a flame;
> The bruised reed He never breaks,
>   Nor scorns the meanest name
>   (Isaac Watts' paraphrase, quoted by C. R. North in
>   his commentary *The Second Isaiah*, 1967, p.109).

In these chapters of Isaiah, two contrasting attitudes to the nations appear. Sometimes the gentiles are seen as wilful idolators, opponents of Yahweh the only true God, guilty adversaries of his people Israel, destined for punishment. In other passages, like the present one, they are seen as pitifully blind, weak, helpless; as broken or fading. In as far as they are rebelling against God, they must be punished. But in as far as they are willing to acknowledge him they can open themselves to his arms of love, and to the arms of love which his people extend.

The world is full of broken reeds and fading flames. Often they disguise themselves, present themselves as strong and aggressive: those are sometimes the most bruised ones. The servant of God is called to a ministry which does not break but binds, does not snuff them out but gently fans.

To put it another way, he is called

to open blind eyes,
to bring the captive out of prison,
to bring those who live in the dark out of the dungeon
(42:7).

There are two further powerful ways to describe not so much positive suffering such as persecution or pain or grief, as negative loss of well being. To be blind is to be helpless, to be at a loss, to be incapable of finding your own way, to be unable to avoid dangers which are quite obvious to sighted people, to lose all independence. To blind someone is one of the most unpleasant punishments that can be imposed on him. We recall the fate of Zedekiah after Jerusalem was captured; the worst thing that the Babylonians could do to the rebel king was to blind him (Jer. 52:11). Perhaps he was still alive among the exiles, still a walking example of the deprivation of blindness.

Then, to be imprisoned is to lose freedom; that, in our culture at least, is one of the most fundamental human rights. Liberty! The prisoner has none. He can make no decisions. He can make no plans. He can take no initiatives. He sits and rots: physically, spiritually, mentally, emotionally. King Jehoiachin, the Babylonians' first royal hostage, had sat in a Babylonian prison for 37 years until he was released a few years previously. Perhaps he was still a walking reminder of what prison does to a man.

Here, however, blindness and imprisonment are two symbols of the circumstances of the nations. The task of the servant is to bring sight and freedom, because sight and freedom are the gifts of the God he serves.

WHAT THE SERVANT NEEDS TO BE WARY OF

The servant of Yahweh is called to minister to people whose persons are bruised, whose life is flickering, who can only cry pleadingly for help. Now it is easy to come to share the weaknesses of people you seek to minister to. When I was a curate, I used to play football with a gang of rough teenagers. Whether or not I had any influence on them, they certainly taught me to play dirtier football! It is easy to be dragged down by the people we are seeking to help. That will not be the case with Yahweh's servant, however. *He will not cry out or lift up his voice, or make himself heard in the street* (42:3). The point of this assertion is not that the servant will not be an extraverted, loud-mouthed showman. *He will not cry out*: the word is the one for a cry of distress. It appears in the exodus story, when the Israelites in Egypt *cried out for help, and their cry under bondage came up to God* (Exod. 2:23).

But Israel is in bondage again, and in their distress in exile they cry out because of their affliction. The prophet himself knew, I think, that someone who is called to minister to people like that can come to be affected by their downcastness. He knew that danger himself, as his account of his call reveals. *'Preach'*, he heard the angel say (40:6—the verb 'cry' is used here, too, in the English translations, but it is a different word from the one for crying in anguish; it means more generally to speak loudly). *'Preach what?'*, Isaiah of the exile replied. 'We, your people, are withered like grass in the summer heat. What is the use of preaching to us?' The prophet felt what his people felt about the situation they were in. (See 40:6-7, where the response which begins in verse 6 'What shall I preach?' continues through to the end of verse 7; verse 8 is then the reply to it. See C. Westermann, *Isaiah 40-66*, 1969, p.41).

But the servant will be able to distance himself, in the right sense, from the afflicted people he has to minister to. So *he will not cry out*. Further, when he is involved in ministering to people who are broken and wavering (42:3), he himself *will not waver or break* (42:4: the verse repeats the words applied to the people in verse 3). They are broken and wavering, but *he will not waver or break until he has established judgement in the world* (42:4). The servant will not contract the weaknesses of those to whom he ministers. He has the personal resources to make a success of his calling. He has the staying power. But he needs to be wary of the pressures he will be under.

WHAT THERE IS TO ENCOURAGE HIM

In fulfilling his calling, he is not merely or finally dependent on people's awareness that they need God's truth, or on their broken and wavering state. Nor is he merely or finally dependent on his own resources; everything does not rest on him.

His final encouragement lies in God himself.

He goes into *God's* world. The one who calls him is

the one who created the heavens and stretched them out,
who spread out the earth with all that comes from it,
who gives breath to the people on it
and life to those who live on it (42:5).

God is sending him into *his* world. That answers an objection
the prophet, or the servant, might have been inclined to
make. These messages often begin with God describing himself in such a way as this, and such introductions generally
seem designed to forestall people's objections. They say to
the hearer, as it were, 'When you listen to this message, if you
find it difficult to accept, don't forget to take account of this
...' Now, Yahweh wants his servant to bring light to the
nations. One objection to that might be, surely God is going
to judge the nations? They are heathen. They do not acknowledge him. They have often persecuted his people. They are
responsible for our being in exile. Surely they are not to
receive the light? Or again, supposing we agree that God *may*
want to bless the nations in this way. Nevertheless, how can
he expect a mere human servant of his to bring light to the
nations? It is too big a task. We could not take that on.

Both those possible objections are forestalled by the reminder that Yahweh is the creator of heaven and earth, of the
world and of man. That means on one hand that the God
who is speaking these words is mighty enough to be able to
ensure that any plan he makes is effective. If he says he is
going to use his servant in a certain way, he can do so. After
all, he did make the universe. He has the power.

Then on the other hand, the fact that he is the creator of
man, the one who breathes his breath into each human being,
implies that he does care for all those who live on earth. He is
not interested in only a few; he created them all. So he is
sending the servant into the world he created, to the creatures
he cares about. That is the servant's first encouragement.

His second is that he goes into God's world because of
God's call. There is in the situation, then, all the potential
that comes from being called by God. *I am Yahweh* (that self-

declaration by God characteristically introduces some solemn statement). *I called you with a righteous purpose. I took you by the hand, I kept you* (42:6; compare 42:1). We have already considered those powerful descriptions of the special relationship that obtains between Yahweh and his servant. He is specially chosen, called, taken by the hand, endowed with God's spirit, upheld, kept. All those things are true of him because of his relationship with God; they are part of God's commitment to him. But they are very relevant as God issues his challenge regarding the servant's commitment to God and his purpose. The servant is not acting on his own initiative or in his own strength, but in all the resources of his special calling and his special relationship.

His third encouragement is that God's call arises out of God's own concern for his glory. *I am Yahweh, that is my name. My glory I give to no other, nor my praise to idols* (42:8). The servant's task is to call the bluff of the Babylonian gods, and in principle that of human religion in general. But will it work? What if they laugh in his face? Yahweh says it will work because of his own personal concern. He is not willing for the worship that ought to be his to be given where it does not belong.

But again, how do we know God is concerned for his glory in this way, and is sufficiently powerful to achieve this? That question expresses precisely the exiles' doubts. The prophet answers it by claiming that the people can know God will fulfil this plan to reveal himself, because he has fulfilled his plans before. He has already shown that he is one who speaks and then acts. He has the power to do what he says he will do. Thus, if he is now declaring what he plans to do through his servant, what he says will come to pass.

Now that earlier things have clearly come about,
I am declaring fresh things.
Before they begin to happen
I make them known to you (42:9).

The prophet refers to an important feature of Israel's experience of God throughout the time she was a political entity. Prophets appeared regularly to declare what God had been doing, was doing, and was going to do. So, for instance, Isaiah of Jerusalem in the eighth century had involved himself in the political policy-making of Ahaz and Hezekiah. He had warned that the Assyrians would chastise Judah. He had declared that they, and other contemporary powers, would eventually see their own downfall. His words came true. Some were coming true before the exiles' own eyes: Babylon was about to fall at the hand of the Medes, as Isaiah had said (see Isaiah 13).

Now, if after an event someone says that he is not surprised, that he had thought it might happen, such a claim is less impressive than if beforehand he had gone on record and committed himself as to what he expected to take place. He can then point out subsequently that it has taken place. It is this that the prophet is claiming for Yahweh here, and it points to a significant difference between him and the other gods.

That point is made by the paragraph which leads into the passage about the servant (see 41:21-29: the chapter divisions in Isaiah 40-55 are more often a hindrance than a help in understanding the prophet's message, and this last paragraph of chapter 41, for instance, is really the beginning of a new chapter). The paragraph again speaks of the dismay which world affairs might cause to the exiles and to the Babylonians. Earlier, the prophet had challenged the Babylonian gods as to who is making these events occur (see 41:1-7). Here, however, the challenge concerns the different question, who can interpret these events? Who can explain events that have already taken place, and who can declare where they are leading?

Present your case, Yahweh says.
Produce your arguments, says the King of Jacob.
Let them produce them and tell us what is going to happen.
Tell us about the nature of previous events,
so that we may give them our attention,
and that we may know their outcome;
or inform us of things to come.
Tell us what is to come about in the future,
so that we may know that you are gods.

Do something, good or ill,
so that we can look at it and see.
It is clear, you and all you do are nothing at all.
The person who chooses you is as disgusting as you are.
I roused a man from the north, and he came.
I roused one from the east, to call on my name.
He has trampled on rulers as if they were clay,
as if he was a potter treading it.
Who announced this from the beginning, so that we could
    know?
Who announced it beforehand, so that we could say he
    was right?
There was no-one who announced it, no-one declared it.
No-one heard you announce anything.
I appoint an advocate for Zion,
I give a herald for Jerusalem.
But I looked, and there was no-one,
among them there was no counsellor
to give an answer when I ask a question.
It is clear that they are idols,
their deeds are nothing,
their images are empty breath (41:21-29).

Yahweh, the God of Israel, is the one who long ago declared
that Babylon would defeat Israel and that the Medes would
defeat Babylon. He shows that he is able to make up his mind
to do something, and then do it. *Earlier things have clearly
come about*; therefore the servant can be encouraged to
believe the *fresh things* (42:9). The servant goes into God's
world by God's call, which arises from God's concern for his
glory and is backed up by the proven power of God's word.

TO WHOM DOES THE SERVANT CALLING APPLY?

The Christian believes that Jesus is the servant par excellence.
But we have begun studying Isaiah 42 without referring to
Jesus, listening to it as if we were the exiles when they heard
the prophet's message for the first time. The exiles have been
reminded that Israel is God's servant, and that this means
God is committed to them (41:8-10). Now they are further
reminded that to be God's servant means that they must be

committed to him.

The story of Israel is the story of how God tried, and failed, to bring that about. His purpose was through Israel to reach the world. But the plan did not work. In an essay on 'Prophecy and Fulfillment' (in a symposium called *Essays on Old Testament Interpretation*, edited by C. Westermann, 1963), Rudolf Bultmann talks about the Old Testament as a whole as the story of the miscarriage of God's plan, the story of God's failure. That was why Jesus had to come, to succeed where Israel failed, so that (in a sense) God could succeed where he had failed before. It is in this sense that he is the servant, par excellence.

It is he, then, who is the light of the world, he who brings a covenant relationship with his father which all men can enjoy. It is he who refuses to snap a broken reed or snuff out a flickering flame: we can see that in his personal caring for people like the failure Peter or the bereaved widow at Nain or the social outcast Zacchaeus or Mary Magdalene. It is he who is never dragged down by the weaknesses of these people who become his friends; he remains a burning and a shining light, he does not waver like a flickering candle. He also retains an unshakeable confidence that God will bring his work to fruition, despite being let down by his people, his family, his friends, and his betrayer.

Jesus's fulfilment of the servant's calling is not the end of its significance, however. The servant's task was to bring light to the nations; Jesus was 'the light to lighten the gentiles'. But as well as saying of himself, 'I am the light of the world' (John 8:12), he also says to his followers, 'You are the light of the world' (Matt. 5:14). 'As the Father sent me, so I send you' (John 20:21). He returns the servant calling to the people of God to whom it first belonged.

These themes are ones we shall return to as we look at subsequent servant passages in Isaiah 40-55. But we can begin to note now that the servant calling needs to be looked at from the perspective of these three audiences. First it is a description of the calling of Israel, and in a sense it is still the calling of Israel. But it is a calling mere men could not fulfil, indeed it depresses us, because, like the Old Testament law, it becomes a description of God's expectations which condemn us for our failure to live up to them. So it becomes a description of the calling of Jesus, which he did live up to. But then it is also a description of the calling of the messianic people, and those who reckon to be members of the messianic people cannot escape its challenge to them.

CHAPTER EIGHT

The blind servant (Isaiah 42:18-48:22)

In the course of describing the servant's position as the one to whom God is committed, and the servant's calling to be committed to God's purpose in the world, Isaiah of the exile has given several hints that actually Israel cannot fulfil the servant's task. There is a tension between the two portraits. For instance, a key aspect of this task is that he should be the means of putting God's judgement into effect, of seeing that God's gracious and wise ordering of the world's affairs is a reality among the nations. But the prophet has referred earlier to God's involvement with people's rights, and there his words concerned Israel's complaint that Yahweh was not looking after *her* rights. We have mentioned already this expression of how she felt in exile: *the path I tread is hidden from Yahweh. My right has passed out of God's notice* (40:27: the word for 'right' is the same as the one translated 'judgement' in 42:1,3,4). The servant's task is to be concerned for God's establishing what is right for people. But Israel is so worried about what is right for herself (naturally enough in the situation) that it seems doubtful whether she will have the personal resources and energy to give herself in concern for what's right for other peoples. Yet that was the servant's task.

Again, the servant is not to *cry out or lift up his voice, or make it heard in the street*. But this is just what Israel is doing when she laments Yahweh's having abandoned her. The servant will be someone who brings strength to broken reeds and fans flickering flames, and someone who does not flicker or break himself. But Israel in exile *is* a broken reed, a flickering flame. The servant is to bring sight to the blind and freedom to the prisoners; but Israel is in bondage, and there are questions which might be asked about her spiritual sight.

So far the prophet has only hinted at this problem. He has said Israel is God's servant, and that is a comfort to her. He has then painted such a picture of what the servant will do that it simply leaves one wondering very seriously whether Israel can fulfil it. But eventually the point becomes explicit.

> *You deaf people, listen!*
> *You blind, look and see!* (42:18)

If the reader has not picked up Isaiah's hints, then he will naturally assume the prophet is speaking to the nations who are spiritually deaf and blind. But if the reader thought that, he is now rudely awakened.

> *Who is blind but my servant?*
> *Who is as deaf as the messenger I send?*
> *Who is as blind as my envoy?*
> *Who is as blind as Yahweh's servant?*
> *You see much, but you do not pay heed to it.*
> *He opens his ears, but he does not listen* (42:19-20).

The point is now quite explicit. Israel has the status of the servant, but not the spiritual sight and hearing which are necessary to someone who is to be God's messenger. She has sight, but not insight. She has heard all about Cyrus, and can put two and two together and see the turmoil he is going to cause shortly in Babylon, but she cannot perceive that this is Yahweh's way of fulfilling *his* purposes. So he cannot fulfil his purpose through her.

> *Yahweh wanted, for the sake of his righteous purpose,*
> *to exalt the teaching and glorify it (42:21).*

The prophet summarizes the purpose of God which the servant had been commissioned to fulfil, a purpose of righteousness in revealing the teaching for which the nations were looking (42:4,6). But he cannot achieve this through Israel. Here is the people who are supposed to embody the splendour of God's revelation and thus to prove it to the nations:

> *But this is a people despoiled and plundered,*
> *trapped in holes, all of them,*
> *hidden in dungeons.*
> *They have become spoil with no-one to rescue it,*
> *plunder with no-one to say 'Give it back' (42:22).*

Further, they lack the insight to see the explanation for their predicament (42:23). In their prayers, it seems, they lamented the fact that they were given over to be pillaged and looted, and no doubt went on (as the Psalms do) to ascribe the responsibility for it to Yahweh. Indeed, they were right. It was Yahweh who had allowed it to happen. But they could not see the clear reason why he had done so.

> *Who gave Jacob to the plunderer and Israel to the*
>   *despoiler?*
> *Was it not Yahweh against whom we sinned,*
> *in whose ways we were not willing to walk,*
> *whose law we did not obey?*
> *So he poured on him the blaze of his anger and the fury of*
>   *war (42:24-25).*

Yahweh wanted to commend his revelation to the world. The way of doing that was to show how well it worked in Israel. But in fact it did not work at all in Israel, because she would not take it seriously. That is the explanation of why Jerusalem was destroyed and why Israel was taken into exile, though it remains an explanation the exiles find it difficult to accept.

> So he poured on him the blaze of his anger and the fury of
>   war.
> It wrapped him in flames, but he did not acknowledge this.
> It burned him, but he did not take it to heart (42:25).

They still cannot see it.

Of course Israel was no more blind or deaf than average. They were behaving in the way that ordinary sinful human beings do. The servant is only typically human. Paul makes that assumption himself when he talks about Israel and the church (Rom. 11). Israel is like an olive tree. When gentiles come to believe in the Messiah, they are like new branches grafted into that olive tree. There is room for so many of them to be grafted in because, fortunately for them, many of the original branches have been pruned out. But, Paul argues, it would be very dangerous if these new branches started to think that they were superior to the ones pruned out. They ought rather to learn humbly from them. Otherwise they risk the same fate themselves.

We ourselves live in an age in which the church often seems blind and in bondage. Compared with days in which it flourished, it is a pathetic minority in a world which totally ignores it. It has little influence on the life of the nation, and little reputation. Even when people start taking an interest in Jesus, it does not necessarily lead them to take an interest in us, the church. Furthermore the church often seems to delight in hiding from the realities of the situation, in pretending that things are not so bad. Or it acknowledges that things are bad and sees this as the result of the world's opposition and sin. That was really what Israel did. But Yahweh reminded her that her exile was not the result merely of the world's resistance to the truth or of his own sleepiness. It was the result of their sin. The state of the church is to be explained not merely in economic or social terms. It raises questions about our attitude to God, as was the case with Israel.

So the servant who was supposed to bring sight to the blind and freedom to the prisoner is, by his own neglect, sightless and in bondage. The natural step for God is therefore to pension him off. In three ways, however, God says 'No' to this possibility. 'No', because I still love him (43:1-7).

'No', because I still intend him to be my servant (43:8-13).
'No', because I am going to restore him (43:14-21 and following sections).

'NO', BECAUSE I STILL LOVE HIM

We have already learned something of God's attitude to
people who are blind and imprisoned or broken and wavering. God has said that he is concerned to bring them sight and
freedom, strength and renewal (42:1-9). He was talking there
about those to whom Israel was supposed to minister. But if
Israel herself comes to have needs like that, then perhaps she
can receive the ministry which people like that need? This is
actually one of the moving aspects of these chapters. Often
the prophet speaks about the needy without specifying who
the needy are. God's ideal was that Israel should be the strong
one, with the resources to bring strength to the weak. But the
fact that he does not keep saying, 'I mean Israel here', 'I mean
the gentiles here', enables his words to be applied as they
need to be, to whoever the strong and the weak are. If Israel
is needy, she can *receive* the ministry that she is supposed to
give.

In practice, the people of God (and those who are particularly called to minister within the people of God, or to embody
its mission to those outside) live with an alternation between
these two pictures of themselves. Their model of ministry or
mission has commonly been the hero or heroine whose relationship with God never falters, whose commitment never
hesitates, whose love never runs out, whose patience never
tires. Their ministry to the weak, the needy, and the doubting
therefore never flags. That model can lead to the belief that
those who minister can never themselves show weakness or
need (and must therefore hide it from themselves and from
others), and this belief has in turn led sometimes to the entire
rejection of the model, as being unreal. That is an over-reac-
tion. Those who minister *are* called to embody that model.
But they remain human and frail, and have weaknesses and
needs, which cannot (and need not) be finally denied or
hidden. The grace of God, which in moments of strength can

be applied to others, in moments of need can be applied to oneself. If we cannot be the Lord's servant dispensing the Lord's strength to the weak, we can be the Lord's servant receiving the Lord's strength for the weak.

Yet one of the consequences of becoming for a time broken and wavering oneself, and in need of being ministered to because one is no longer in a state to minister, is that one is no longer capable of applying the promises and the grace of God to oneself (let alone to others). This was certainly the situation of the exiles. The prophet brings them no new message. He merely reminds them of old truths about God as their creator and their sovereign and their 'guardian', old truths which are embodied in the story of their history and in the praise of their psalms. They are quite familiar with these; yet they have quite forgotten them. They are no longer able to take them into account. So the servant who is weak and unable to serve has to be ministered to. This perhaps implies that when the servant is strong he or she has to be concerned not only to minister to the weak, but also to ensure that there are ways that one can be ministered to when one is weak. One needs people to whom one can go, or one needs to know what parts of Scripture to direct oneself to in such circumstances. There have to be ways in which the servant can receive ministry when he or she is in no state to minister.

Indeed, Yahweh promises this to his servant.

> But now this is the word of Yahweh,
> the one who created you, Jacob,
> the one who formed you, Israel:
> Do not be afraid, I have redeemed you.
> I called you by name. You belong to me.
> When you pass through the sea, I will be with you.
> When you pass through the rivers, they will not
>   overwhelm you.
> When you walk through fire you will not be touched,
> the flame will not burn you.
> Because I, Yahweh, am your God,
> I, the holy one of Israel, am your deliverer,
> I give Egypt as your ransom,
> Sudan and Ethiopia in return for you.
> Because you are precious in my eyes,

because of the honour you have and because I love you,
I give men in return for you,
I give peoples in return for your life.
Do not be afraid, I am with you.
I will bring your descendants from the east,
I will gather you from the west,
I will say to the north, 'Give them up',
and to the south, 'Do not hold them back'.
'Bring my sons from far away,
bring my daughters from the end of the earth,
everyone who calls himself by my name,
whom I created, whom I formed,
whom I made, for my glory' (43:1-7).

The prophet reiterates what he has said previously about Yahweh's purpose to restore Israel (compare especially 41: 8-20). He begins and ends with the assertion that it was Yahweh who created Israel in the first place, to be his in a special sense (43:1,7). That is a further reason for their believing that he really will look after them and bring them back; burning and captivity (42:22,24,25) are not his last word to them (43:2,5-6). He would give anything for them (43:3b-4). And at the base of these promises and these declarations is fundamentally a relationship between him and them and an attitude on his part that values and honours and loves them (43:2-3a). Some of these expressions are new, but even where the words are the same as they have been earlier, it is not mere repetition, for the previous paragraph which spoke of Israel's blindness and deafness (42:18-25) was an accusation. The words and the style would be familiar to the prophet's hearers from everyday life. It is an accusation, and the accused has no scope for self-defence. There is no doubt that the elders gathered at the city gate would declare that the case was proven. So all there is to follow is the sentencing. Israel has rebelled against Yahweh and failed to show the slightest insight even when she has been chastised. Therefore . . . .

But this is not what follows. The prophet's next word (43:1) is not 'therefore'; it is 'but'. 'But' is one of the important recurrent introductions to the grace and the power of God as the Bible speaks of it. What is quite unexpected, humanly speaking, comes about by God's power (for instance, Acts

2:24), God's mercy (Eph. 2:24), God's providence (Gen. 50:20). So it is here. The sentence which one expects will follow incontrovertible guilt is not passed. Instead Yahweh's commitment to his people is re-asserted. 'You are still the one I chose and called by name, the one I love. I am with you.' God re-iterates this after he and his people have together looked further into the depth of his people's blindness, deafness, and uselessness to him. He hides from none of the truth about Israel, indeed he brings it all out into the open, and then declares, 'But I still love you.'

If that was the word of God to the exiles in the sixth century B.C. it has at least two sets of implications for the twentieth century A.D. One is its implications for the actual descendants of Old Testament Israel, for the Jewish people. Isaiah of the exile declared that God was committed to Israel no matter what happened, despite their sin. This is often not how the Christian church has looked at the Jewish people. A terrible toll of Christian persecution of Jewish people has been exacted over the past two millennia, and remains on the conscience of the church of Christ. The church has seen the Jews as the crucifiers of Jesus, but not as the people of God to whom God is irrevocably committed.

That commitment is not only an Old Testament belief. Paul believes that the Jews in his day are the objects of God's wrath, because they have rejected and killed the Messiah and try to stifle the messianic gospel (1 Thess. 1:16): like Isaiah of the exile, he speaks as a Jew to Jews, and his understanding of the position of the Jews is similar to that of the prophet. But also like the prophet, Paul declares that nevertheless God is still committed to Israel, even though she refuses to commit herself to the Messiah—because 'the gifts and the call of God are irrevocable' (Rom. 11:29). That phrase could be a summary of the gospel according to Isaiah in the exile: all Paul does in his theological discussion of the place of the Jews is re-state that message in the light of the shock of the Jews' rejection of Jesus. That will not be the end, Paul says; God is still committed to Israel, so the time will come when they recognize their Messiah. For God still loves them. They may not escape the fire and the flood unharmed (as the exiles were promised they would, 43:2); but God still goes with them through the

fire and the flood, and even brings new birth out of holocaust.
Still he says to them, *You belong to me* (43:1).

That relationship and the promises that issue from it remain
real for the actual descendants of the exiles. They are given
new extent and depth in the gospel of Christ for all who
believe in him, both Jew and Gentile. In John's Gospel, Jesus
makes this point by describing himself as the good shepherd,
caring not only for his accustomed (Jewish) flock, but also for
other sheep beyond that. They are secure with him; no-one
can snatch them from his hand, still less from the hand of his
Father (John 10:14,16,28,29). That image takes us back to
Isaiah, for here the Lord returning to Jerusalem is pictured
not only as a victorious warrior, but also as a caring shepherd:

Like a shepherd he tends his flock,
he gathers the lambs with his arm,
he carries them in his arms,
he leads the ewes to water (40:11).

... and no-one is able to snatch them out of the Father's hand.
No matter how unworthy we may seem, no matter how unworthy we may really become, God says to us all, 'You are
still the one I chose, the one I called by name, the one I love.
Do not be afraid, I am with you.' And even when he and we
have together looked at our blindness and deafness and uselessness, he still declares, 'But I love you all the same.'

'NO', BECAUSE I STILL INTEND TO USE HIM AS MY SERVANT

The blind and deaf servant is not to be cast off, not only
because God still loves him, but also because God has not
abandoned the plan to use him. In the re-iteration of Israel's
relationship with God at which we have been looking, one
note is conspicuous by its absence. 'Fear not, I am with you, I
have redeemed you, I am your God ...' But one crucial description of Israel is missing. She is not described as God's
servant.

It would perhaps have been a quite understandable com-
promise on God's part. He would keep his commitment to

Israel by still regarding her as his people. He would still
restore her, still redeem her, still keep her in his arms of love.
But he would realistically acknowledge that it did not really
seem possible to use her as his servant, his means of revealing
himself and fulfilling his purpose in the world. She would not
be sacked, but she would be kicked upstairs.

That possibility is now ruled out by what follows, however.

> *Bring out the people that are blind, though they have eyes,*
> *that are deaf, though they have ears.*
> *All the nations have gathered together,*
> *the peoples have assembled.*
> *Who among them could have announced this,*
> *could have told us of the events which are now past?*
> *Let them produce their witnesses to prove them right,*
> *so that people may hear and say, 'It is true'.*
> *You are my witnesses, Yahweh says,*
> *you are my servant whom I chose,*
> *so that you may know and trust in me,*
> *so that you might see that I am the one.*
> *Before me no god was formed,*
> *and after me there will be none.*
> *It is I, I am Yahweh,*
> *and there is no deliverer apart from me.*
> *It was I who announced it, I delivered you,*
> *I declared it, and there was no stranger among you.*
> *And you are my witnesses, Yahweh says.*
> *I am God; in the future too, I am the one.*
> *There is no-one who can take things from my hand.*
> *I act, and who can reverse it? (43:8-13).*

The servant is deaf and the witnesses are blind, but Yahweh
still wants witnesses, because he needs someone to testify to
his sole lordship of history, and he still intends that Israel
should act as his witnesses, his servant. Indeed, the prophet
says, he is telling them that Israel is still to act as God's
servant, because this in itself will lead to the building up of
their faith.

It is possible that the prophet has in mind here the striking
fact that having to function as God's witness builds up his
servant's faith in him. This is certainly true in experience. I

think that what he means is something slightly different, however. It is rather that his actually telling Israel that she is still
his servant, still his witnesses, is a means of building up her
faith in him, because it is difficult to imagine how God could
say anything that was more gracious, more loving, and more
calculated to win her love and response to him. He says to
her, 'I know you are blind, I know you are deaf, I know you
are in prison. I know you are finding it more and more difficult
to believe in me, and to believe that I care about you. So how
can I encourage your faith, how can I win your response?
Can I do it by telling you this? If I am to reveal myself to the
world I need someone to be my servant, my witnesses. That
is the most important role I could give to anyone. And I am
giving it to you. *Now* do you believe that I am committed to
you?'

Again, if those were God's words to the exiles in the sixth
century B.C., they are suggestive with regard to the position
of both the Jewish people and the Christian church in the
twentieth century A.D. God's commitment to Israel, his
irrevocable gifts and calling, consist not merely in Israel's still
being his chosen one. It means that God still intends to use
Israel as his servant and his witnesses. Paul also takes up this
aspect of God's commitment to Israel. He not only asserts
that Israel is going to be saved. He also declares that Israel is
again to be a means of blessing to the world. It is because of
Israel's rejection of the Messiah that the apostles came to concentrate on bringing the good news of Jesus to the gentiles
(see Acts 13:44-49). But 'if their trespass means riches for the
world, and if their failure means riches for the Gentiles, how
much more will their full inclusion mean! ... If their rejection
means the reconciliation of the world, what will their acceptance mean but life from the dead?' (Rom. 11:12,15 RSV). The
words are vague; Paul is not precise in the way he speaks
here. But he implies that there is a further role for his servant
Israel yet to fulfil as his witness in the world.

But the Gentile-Jewish Christian church also inherits God's
Old Testament promises. To them, too, he says that he does
not go back on making people his servants. We can go back
on our commitment to God. We can slide gradually away
from him and commit acts that are quite unworthy of him.

We can seem to ourselves unforgivable and unrestorable, as those who have gone too far away and have sullied ourselves too much. But to his disobedient, faithless, hopeless people God still says, *You are my witnesses ... you are my servant ..., so that you may know and trust in me ...* (43:10).

Paradoxically, of course, in a sense we will be able to prove God's grace even more convincingly than we could before, because we demonstrate that God's love for people is totally and solely dependent on himself and not at all on their qualifications. Thus, however far away from him we may drift, we are never disqualified from being his servants or his witnesses, because the reason for our being his witnesses never did lie in our qualifications. It lay in his choice, and that choice stands. God still says, *You are my witnesses.*

'NO', BECAUSE I AM GOING TO RESTORE HIM

Isaiah of the exile goes on to add (and to develop at some length) a further response to the question whether the imprisoned and blind servant is to be cast off. Those experiences of imprisonment and blindness suggest two different problems which the prophet (and Yahweh) have to face. The one is more outward and material, the other more inward and spiritual.

So far many of the prophecies have been quite general, even vague. We have assumed that the warrior from the east is Cyrus, that his people are the Persians, that it is the Babylonians that they threaten, and so on, but none of these parties has been actually named. Now the picture starts to come into focus as the prophet declares how the exiles' outward, material, political problem will be dealt with.

> *These are the words of Yahweh,*
> *your redeemer, the holy one of Israel:*
> *For your sake I have sent to Babylon,*
> *and I will lay them prostrate as fugitives, all of them,*
> *the Chaldaeans in the ships they exult in* (43:14).

The agent of this act, King Cyrus himself, is soon named in turn for the first time.

Thus says Yahweh, your redeemer,
he who formed you in the womb:
I, myself, Yahweh, made all things ...
I am he who says of Cyrus, 'My shepherd—
he will fulfil my whole purpose,
saying of Jerusalem, "Let her be rebuilt",
and of the Temple, "Let your foundation be laid" '.
Thus says Yahweh to his anointed, to Cyrus,
whom he has taken by his right hand
to subdue nations before him
and strip the loins of kings,
to force gateways before him
that their gates be closed no more:
I will go before you
levelling the heights.
I will shatter the bronze gateways,
smash the iron bars.
I will give you the hidden treasures,
the secret hoards,
that you may know that I am Yahweh,
the God of Israel, who calls you by your name (44:24,28;
    45:1-3 JB).

Cyrus is Yahweh's anointed (45:1). That is a rather extraordinary statement. The Hebrew word for 'anointed' is
'Messiah'. The 'anointed one', the 'Messiah', is in the time
before the exile the king of David's line. When there is no
king of David's line, the Messiah is the Davidic king that
people hope will occupy that throne in the future. But Isaiah
of the exile is so convinced that Cyrus is (unknown to himself) Yahweh's agent that he sees him as the fulfilment of the
hopes of the Messiah.

It was Cyrus, too, who would expose the impotence of the
Babylonian gods. They are in turn now named for the first
time.

Bel has crouched down, Nebo has stooped low:
their images, once carried in your processions,
have been loaded on to beasts and cattle,
a burden for the weary creatures;
they stoop and they crouch;

> not for them to bring the burden to safety;
> the gods themselves go into captivity (46:1-2 NEB).

The gods that were formerly carried in procession are carried to safety when the city's downfall is imminent (actually their priests stayed in Babylon and changed sides when Cyrus arrived, but perhaps that act makes their gods' impotence even clearer). The prophet enjoys bringing out the irony of the scene: 'I thought that your gods were supposed to support you, not that you had to support your gods!' At least Yahweh can carry his people:

> Listen to me, house of Jacob
> and all the remnant of the house of Israel,
> a load on me from your birth, carried by me from the
>   womb:
> till you grow old I am He,
> and when white hairs come, I will carry you still;
> I have made you and I will bear the burden,
> I will carry you and bring you to safety (46:3-4 NEB).

The prophet goes on to describe Babylon herself as a woman who was once so fine, so stately, so impressive, so proud, but is now humiliated and exiled as Israel had once been (see Isaiah 47). Thus, Israel can go free:

> Come out of Babylon!
> Run from the Chaldaeans!
> Shout out the news, proclaim this message,
> send it out to the ends of the earth,
> say, Yahweh has redeemed his servant Jacob! (48:20).

Isaiah of the exile thus offers Israel encouragement after encouragement about the physical restoration of the people. Cyrus will arrive, Babylon will be defeated, the exiles will return home, Jerusalem will be restored. The exiles are in bondage, in prison. But they are to be released.

At the same time as one reads these repeated promises of restoration, however, one notices another contrasting aspect of their need emerging. From the beginning of these prophecies, it is true, Israel has been described as demoralized,

her faith exhausted, her hope gone, her spirit unable to com-
prehend what Yahweh is doing with her. She was very needy.
But she was not actively rebellious. But as these promises
unfold, and the message of restoration is expounded, a surprising feature emerges. Israel seems to be resisting God's
word. She now seems to be rebellious.

This is hinted at in the urgent way the prophet has to repeat
his messages. We have noted that he declares that Israel could
not really be God's servant because of her sin, but that nevertheless God is still committed to her, still wants her as his
witnesses, and still plans to restore her (42:18-43:21). But
then he repeats the whole message, point by point, with
perhaps greater emphasis (43:22-45:8). In the light of what
follows, the reason for this seems to be that he found that the
exiles would not listen to his message. It had to be repeated
and re-emphasized.

The exiles are not merely reluctant to listen to the message;
they are actively resistant to it. The prophet declared that he
was going to use Cyrus to restore Israel. He was Yahweh's
anointed. It seems that in some quarters this was a very un-
welcome message. It was almost as if someone began to talk
about King Hussein of Jordan as the Messiah. So the prophet
has to deal with those who resist his message.

Does a clay pot dare to argue with its maker,
a pot that is like all the others?
Does the clay ask the potter what he is doing?
Does the pot complain that its maker has no skill?
Does anyone dare to say to his parents,
"Why did you make me like this?"
The LORD, the holy God of Israel,
the one who shapes the future, says:
"You have no right to question me about my children
or tell me what I ought to do!
I am the one who made the earth
and created mankind to live there.
By my power I stretched out the heavens;
I control the sun, the moon, and the stars.
I myself have stirred Cyrus to action
to fulfil my purpose and put things right.
I will straighten every road that he travels.

He will rebuild my city, Jerusalem,
and set my captive people free.
No one has hired him or bribed him to do this."
The LORD Almighty has spoken (45:9-13 GNB).

The message about the exposure of the Babylonian gods also
leads in to a challenge to those who oppose his message.

Remember this and take it to heart.
Recall it to mind, you rebels ...
Listen to me, you stubborn-hearted,
you who are so far away from my righteous purpose.
I have brought my righteous purpose near, it is not far
    away ... (46:8,12,13).

The point comes out most clearly after the chapter which describes the humiliation of Babylon herself.

Listen to this, people of Israel,
you that are descended from Judah:
You swear by the name of the LORD
and claim to worship the God of Israel—
but you don't mean a word you say.
And yet you are proud to say
that you are citizens of the holy city
and that you depend on Israel's God,
whose name is the LORD Almighty.
The LORD says to Israel,
"Long ago I predicted what would take place,
then suddenly I made it happen.
I knew that you would prove to be stubborn,
as rigid as iron and unyielding as bronze.
And so I predicted your future long ago,
announcing events before they took place,
to prevent you from claiming
that your idols and images made them happen.
All I foretold has now taken place;
you have to admit my predictions were right.
Now I will tell you of new things to come,
events that I did not reveal before.
Only now am I making them happen;
nothing like this took place in the past.

If it had, you would claim that you knew all about it.
I knew that you couldn't be trusted,
that you have always been known as a rebel.
That is why you never heard of this at all,
why no word of it ever came to your ears.
In order that people will praise my name,
I am holding my anger in check;
I am keeping it back and will not destroy you.
I have tested you in the fire of suffering,
as silver is refined in a furnace.
But I have found that you are worthless ..."
"If only you had listened to my commands!
Then blessings would have flowed for you
like a stream that never goes dry!
Victory would have come to you
like the waves that roll on the shore.
Your descendants would be as numerous as grains of sand,
and I would have made sure they were never destroyed ..."
"There is no safety for sinners," says the LORD
(48:1-10,18-19,22 GNB).

So the prophet makes it more and more explicit and clear
how Israel is to be restored nationally and politically through
Cyrus. But he also makes Israel's inner problem more and
more clear. Through his being sent to tell the exiles how their
material needs were to be met, there comes to the surface the
exiles' loss of faith, their inability to learn, their slowness to
turn to God, their resistance to God's will, the unreality of
their profession of response to God, their spiritual obstinacy,
their cynicism, their inclination to place their trust anywhere
but in him.

There is no 'shalom' for rebels (48:22). In the church today,
there is much talk of *shalom*, that wholeness in all aspects of
human life which is God's purpose for man. *Shalom* includes
both the material and the spiritual, and it is easy for one or
other of these to become all-important. The witness of Isaiah
40-55 is that God cares about his people's outward welfare,
but that it is possible to be restored to one's land and to have
a new Jerusalem and a new temple, without having a new
heart. If the people of God find outward success but no
inward renewal, they do not find real *shalom*. Cyrus is to

bring the exiles back to Palestine, but who will bring them back to God? Before Israel can function as God's servant, she needs someone to fulfil a servant ministry to her. So who is to be a servant for Israel?

CHAPTER NINE

The persistent servant (Isaiah 49-50)

Isaiah 40-48 reveals Yahweh's plan for bringing Israel back to Palestine, and declares that the plan is in process of fulfilment. But it also raises more and more sharply the question how Israel is to be brought back to God. How can she find the real *shalom* which is impossible for rebels against God (48:22)?

It is this task which we are now told is to be fulfilled by Yahweh's servant. Yahweh *formed me in the womb to be his servant, to bring Jacob back to him, so that Israel might be gathered to him* (49:5). It is the calling of the Lord's servant to bring Israel back to the Lord.

Now we have noted that scholars have puzzled endlessly over who the prophet means by the servant in Isaiah 40-55. Sometimes it is explicit that Israel is the servant (for instance, 41:8-10 and 44:1-2), and I have suggested that elsewhere, too, in the chapters we have looked at, the natural view is that Israel is meant to be the servant (notably 42:1-9). The servant is supposed to be Israel; yet this servant is blind and imprisoned (42:18-25). She cannot fulfil the servant's task, and someone has to be a servant *to* Israel. The problem about understanding who Isaiah means by the servant arises out of that complication: Israel *is* the servant, but Israel needs a servant to minister to her, as the prophet now makes explicit.

So who is this servant who is to minister to Israel?

> *Listen to me, coastlands!*
> *Pay heed, distant peoples!*
> *Yahweh called me before I was born.*
> *When I was still in my mother's womb he named my name.*
> *He made my mouth like a sharp sword*
> *and hid me in his hand.*
> *He made me a polished arrow*
> *and concealed me in his quiver.*
> *He said to me, 'You are my servant ...' (49:1-3).*

Words like those are familiar enough from the testimonies of prophets. These particular words are especially reminiscent of Jeremiah's account of how Yahweh called him to be a prophet: how he formed him for this purpose from the womb and put his words in Jeremiah's mouth (Jer. 1:5,9). It is a prophet who is speaking here, Isaiah of the exile talking about his own calling and ministry.

For this prophet himself has been seeking to minister to Israel. He has also been seeking to understand what God is doing with her, and to perceive what are her needs. He has seen more and more clearly that she needs someone to minister to her before she can minister to others. Perhaps he has asked himself, 'How is Yahweh going to meet these inner needs of Israel so that she can serve him again? How is he going to bring Israel back to himself?'. Perhaps it was now like a shattering realization dawning. *He* was the one Yahweh was going to use. Of course it is often the case that the person who perceives a need and comes to be burdened about something is the person the Lord is going to use to meet that need. There is a certain risk involved in becoming too interested in and concerned in this way: it can turn out to be part of God's preparation of his servant.

So here (in Isa. 49:1-6) we are being given a description of the calling and ministry of a man whom God purposes to use as his servant to the servant, the one who will minister to the deepest needs of the people of God in exile. Shortly (in Isa. 50:4-9) we are given a further testimony concerning his experience in fulfilling this calling. Together, these two passages suggest various insights on what it means to be Yahweh's servant.

HE IS ONE WHO IS PREPARED BY GOD

Yahweh called me before I was born. When I was still in my mother's womb he named my name (49:1). We have already considered Jeremiah's account of his call, where the words are similar. The prophet is expressing the conviction that Yahweh's involvement with him goes back to the beginning of his life, and beyond that to his very formation as a person. Yahweh knew even then what role he had in mind for him, and from the beginning he prepared him for it.

God knows even the ways in which he is going to have to modify his plans in the light of the interplay between his own purpose and the attitudes of those he seeks to use. We ourselves are used to the experience of things not turning out as we planned; we do our best to anticipate what may go wrong with our schemes, but we accept that unforeseen obstacles are nevertheless bound to arise. We shall need to revise our plans and adapt them as we are implementing them. In one sense, God himself also does that: the prophet's calling to be the servant arises from the revision of God's plan in the light of the exiles' resistance to his message. But God can anticipate the obstacles his plans will experience, and he can allow for their revision even before they are implemented. So the prophet's call to be the servant is not a hasty botching of an imperfect scheme. It had been allowed for, and he had been prepared for it even before the snag had actually manifested itself. So when unexpected things happen to God's servants or they have to be drafted in to fill sudden gaps, they may still be involved in the outworking of what God had planned long ago. Further, if God knows from the beginning how he plans to use his servants in particular situations then this implies that he can take account of each event and experience in their lives as these unfold. No 'accidents' happen to them. All that they experience is taken account of by the God who knows about it before they are born.

God prepares his servant for the specific task he has in mind for him. *He made my mouth like a sharp sword and hid me in his hand. He made me a polished arrow and concealed me in his quiver* (49:2). From the beginning of his life he was prepared, like a sword made ready in its sheath, or like an arrow in its quiver waiting to be used. The comparison with a sword or an arrow suggests that the prophet does not understand his ministry to be confined to a message of comfort (despite 40:1). Or perhaps he now recognizes, as he did not previously, that the message has to be confrontational in order to bring real comfort. He is himself in the midst of experiencing resistance to his message, even though it is a message of good news. He meets resistance for various reasons: people did not like the way God proposed to go about restoring his people, they found the message too good to be true, they discovered that they had to face up to some uncomfortable truths about themselves. Despite the message of comfort, Isaiah of the exile had to be confrontational. He brought not peace, but a sword. But he knew that he had been prepared for that. As a servant of God, he was one with whom God had been involved from the beginning of his life as the Lord of the events and experiences of his life even before his calling, which had all played their part in preparing him for the particular task God had in mind for him.

As we noted in the case of Jeremiah, this could seem like a tyranny: 'I am not free to make my own decisions, I am merely a cog in a wheel.' But for Isaiah of the exile it is, on the contrary, a valuable reassurance when he is under pressure. He took on a ministerial role among the exiles which brought its cost to him personally and which seemed rather unsuccessful. But it was all within the providence and purpose of a loving God who does not make mistakes. Yahweh planned this role for him; he is in the right place.

HE IS ONE WHO WILL LIVE UP TO WHAT IT MEANS TO BE ISRAEL

*He said to me, 'You are my servant,
you are Israel in whom I shall take pride' (49:3).*

Here are three descriptions of the prophet. 'You are my servant.' There is nothing very surprising about a prophet being described in this way. In the Old Testament, kings and prophets are regularly described as God's servant, and Isaiah of Jerusalem spoke of himself in these terms (Isa. 20:3). On the other hand, all that has been said about the calling of God's servant so far in these chapters adds to the dimensions of what God now means when he says to the prophet, 'You are my servant'.

Even so, we are not prepared for the surprise of what then follows. *'You are my servant, you are Israel.'* Some scholars have found it so surprising that the prophet should identify himself with Israel that they have concluded that this must be a mistake which crept in as the scribes went about their task of copying down the text of the book of Isaiah. But that is rather too easy a way to dispose of a surprising statement. We ought to try to make sense of it as it stands. It surely reflects the prophet's discovery that Israel in exile is not really capable at the moment of living up to what it means to be Israel. To be Israel is to be God's own possession, a kingdom of priests and a holy nation (Exod. 19:5-6). It is to be a people who love, trust, obey, serve, and fear the living God. It is to be a people open to God's blessing and keen to reflect him to the world. But Israel as a whole cannot be those things at the moment. The outward Israel does not have the real Israel's characteristics.

This is not a new situation. It happened, for instance, in the time of Elijah and in the time of Jeremiah. Now at moments like that only individuals such as those prophets seem to behave like Israel. Isaiah of the exile is one of that line. He alone gives God the response which the real Israel gives. He is the real Israel. *You are my servant, you are Israel... ... in whom I shall take pride.* Israel was supposed to be the body that the Lord took pride in (44:23). The prophet uses a word that refers, for instance, to a woman's finery. God wants to parade Israel before the world and before the other so-called gods, and say, as it were, 'Are you not impressed by this achievement of mine?' But the way Israel has behaved has made him unable to do that. God's desire is nearer to fulfilment in the life of the prophet himself, however. He has opened himself to insight into Yahweh's purpose. He has sought to serve him. He is willing to be one of whom Yahweh can be proud.

When Paul expresses for himself the conviction held by

Jeremiah and by Isaiah of the exile that God had set him apart
for his service even before he was born, he goes on to describe
his actual conversion and calling as the revealing of God's
Son *in* him (Gal. 1:15-16). It was not merely a revelation *to*
Paul, but something that came to be embodied *in* his life, so
that from then on God was revealed *through* him. Isaiah of
the exile, too, is to be the means of God's message reaching
his contemporaries. But this comes about in part through his
being the embodiment of what Israel is herself called to be.
He *is* the servant, Israel in whom God can take pride; this is a
means to his ministering to Israel as she is, so that she herself
can be restored to this calling. God's servants are called to
embody what it means to be God's people, to incarnate what
they are calling God's people to. It is a solemn task. But
Calvin, in his comment on this verse, also notes that it should
be an encouragement. 'This is a very high honour conferred
on poor, feeble men, when the Lord appoints them, though
corrupt and depraved, to promote his glory; and therefore
we ought to be the more encouraged to render to him our service and obedience' (*Commentary on the Book of the Prophet
Isaiah*, Volume IV, 1957, p.12). The servant is someone who
is called to embody what it means to be Israel; he will live up
to that calling.

HE IS ONE IN WHOM HOPE, IN THE END, WINS THE VICTORY OVER DESPAIR

> But I said, 'I have worked to no purpose,
> I have spent my strength to achieve absolutely nothing'
> (49:4).

The prophet surveys the ministry we have been considering.
What is there to show for it? What fruit has he seen? It seems,
none. All he gets is looks of incredulity and words of disbelief. His whole ministry as he reviews it seems to have been
pointless, useless, futile. If he had never taken up his task, it
would not have made a whit of difference to where the exiles
were in relation to God. Like the exiles, he is a broken reed, a
wavering flame. He has, after all, succumbed to the weaknesses of those he was called to minister to.

That is what is threatened. But the prophet does not let this voice of despair have the last word. Related to the servant's own need for ministry is the importance of arguing with oneself when one is under pressure. As we saw in the case of Jeremiah, the doubts and agonies inside have to be expressed; it is not necessary or wise to bottle them up. But then they have to be examined critically. When the servant of God is inclined to think that his work is pointless and useless he has to stand back and ask what other factors need to be taken into account, which he may be ignoring, if he is to come to a balanced judgement.

The trouble with Israel was that when she was broken and fading she had failed to look at her situation from God's perspective. She had stopped taking him into account. She believed that the Lord was no longer concerned about justice for her (40:27). The prophet does not fall into that trap. He applies to himself the message he had delivered earlier. Yahweh does bring judgement, he is concerned that people should enjoy his just purpose being put into effect (42:1,3,4). So here he declares,

> Yet my judgement is in Yahweh's hands,
> my reward is in God's hands (49:4).

My judgement is a word we have looked at earlier (40:27; 42:1,3,4). Israel doubted if Yahweh was any longer concerned to implement a purpose for her, and therefore she was unable to be the means of Yahweh's revealing to the nations what is his purposeful judgement for men. The prophet does not fall into this disbelief, however. Yahweh is in control.

How does he know? If we are to take account of his own message as he has delivered it earlier, it is surely because he has looked at what Yahweh has said and done in the past. Yahweh has shown that he is faithful. He will honour his servant again. He is God's servant, and in him hope, in the end, wins the victory over despair, because the afflictions of his present experience are not allowed to erase from his mind the grounds for confidence in God which his own previous experience and his knowledge of God's dealings with his people have given him.

HE IS ONE WITH A TASK IN RELATION TO
THE PEOPLE OF GOD AND IN RELATION TO THE WORLD

The prophet goes on to refer to three tasks which Isaiah 40-55 as a whole is concerned with.

> *But now this is the word of Yahweh,*
> *who formed me in the womb to be his servant,*
> *to bring Jacob back to him,*
> *so that Israel might be gathered to him,*
> *so that I am honoured in Yahweh's sight*
> *and my God is my strength (49:5).*

The first task is to bring Israel back to God, the task that remains unfulfilled when Cyrus brings her back to Palestine. It is this calling that the prophet here tells us he realizes God gives him. He himself has been identified by the name Israel, because at present the empirical Israel, the Israel that can be seen, does not deserve the name. But the name still belongs to her, and the servant's task is to embody in his own life what it means to be Israel, but then to be involved in ministry to the Israel that can be seen, so that she can become the real Israel.

It is this task which the prophet has been having his doubts about. He is not sure he is getting anywhere. He is having to argue with himself over whether Yahweh is really going to prosper his ministry. Now, if one were allowed to speak in the council of Yahweh, one might want to suggest that the prophet should be given some relief from this task if he cannot be given more support in it. But this is not Yahweh's reaction when the prophet says he is feeling the pressure. On the contrary, the Lord increases the dimensions of what he expects Isaiah of the exile to achieve.

But first, Yahweh refers to the second of the tasks Isaiah 40-55 as a whole is concerned with, but which is not the business of his servant.

> *He says, It is too slight a task for you to be my servant*
> *to re-establish the tribes of Jacob*
> *and bring back what has been preserved of Israel (49:6).*

Re-establishing the tribes of Jacob and bringing back the preserved of Israel to their own land is what we have referred to as the material, political aspect to Israel's restoration. She is to be brought out of bondage and re-established in her own land, but that will all be achieved by means of Cyrus, the foreign king. It is really not at all the most important task there is to do. The Persians can and will achieve that. It is too slight and unimportant a task for God's servant.

The note the prophet strikes here sounds an unfashionable one. We have noted that often Christians have not shown enough interest and involvement in political matters, while at other times they have become over-preoccupied with these questions. It is difficult to get a balanced view of their importance. A balance involves neither underemphasizing nor overemphasizing them. At the moment many Christians are placing considerable stress on them. The view of Isaiah of the exile is that they are important, but that they are the distinctive concern of the secular authorities, not that of the servant of Yahweh. To translate his view into Christian terms, he might hold that it was appropriate for Christians to be involved in politics and in government, as human beings concerned for the fair and efficient management of the world God created. But this involvement is not the task of the ministry or of the church as the church. That is too slight a task compared on the one hand with the challenge of being concerned for the relationship between God's people and God himself (verse 5) and on the other hand with the third task he now speaks of.

> I shall appoint you as a light to the nations
> so that my salvation may reach the ends of the earth
>   (49:6).

One way in which this will come about is indirect. We have seen already that when Israel really becomes Israel, this is to have a shattering effect on the world. So if the prophet as Yahweh's servant exercises an effective ministry in bringing Israel back to God and enabling her really to function as Israel, then his ministry is going to affect the world, too, in an undirect way.

It probably also affects the world in a direct way. Perhaps we are to imagine him preaching to the Babylonians themselves as well as to the exiles. Certainly he has brought light to many generations since, whatever he actually did in his lifetime. And certainly his words became part of the rationale for the first Christians' preaching to the gentiles. The New Testament includes only one direct quotation from these two first-person testimonies of the prophet as servant (49:1-6 and 50:4-9), and it refers the passage not to Jesus but to the ministry of the apostles. Paul and Barnabas were preaching in the synagogue and to gentile crowds in Antioch, in Turkey. The Jews are displeased at the impact they are having among the gentiles, but Paul justifies his turning to the gentiles by quoting this text: 'For so the Lord commanded us, "I have appointed you to be a light for the nations, so that you may bring salvation to the end of the earth" ' (Acts 13:47). Paul finds the pattern for his Christian ministry in the prophet's description of his call. He, too, failed with the Jews, and the prophet's testimony suggests that he turns his attention to the gentiles. The servant is one with a task in relation to Israel and to the world.

HE IS ONE WHO LISTENS IN ORDER THAT HE CAN SPEAK

After that first testimony of the prophet as servant, he reverts for a while to messages of reassurance to Israel and to accounts of how Israel (or rather Zion—Jerusalem personified) finds it so difficult to believe that Yahweh is still concerned for her (49:7 - 50:3). But then he begins to speak again of his own calling (50:4-11). We have seen already that he was prepared for a ministry which would involve words that were sharp, penetrating, and confrontational. Here the words he speaks of are less confrontational, more supportive.

> *The Lord Yahweh has given me a disciple's tongue,*
> *so that I could know how to support the weary.*
> *With a word he arouses me in the morning,*
> *in the morning he arouses my hearing,*
> *so that I listen like a disciple (50:4).*

It is easy for a man full of words to increase rather than relieve someone's weariness. This was true of Job's so-called comforters. They had been at their best when they sat silently with Job, almost in the manner of the family and friends of a Jew 'sitting shiva' with him in a time of bereavement. But when Job's friends opened their mouths, it was to add to rather than to alleviate his affliction. There is a time not to speak.

The art and ministry of listening has been rightly stressed in recent years in connection with counselling. But there is a time to speak. When we have come to understand the precise nature of someone's weariness, our privilege and responsibility is not only to show them that we share it, but also to apply the gospel to it. If we fail to add speaking to our listening, then our silence is guilty. To express sympathy and say how sorry you are may be useless. But that does not mean there are no words to say.

Clearly Isaiah of the exile needed precisely the right message in order to speak to his contemporaries' needs. The key to his having them is the fact that he listens for them. The secret is to have a disciple's tongue, a mouth that speaks what the ears have learned. The teacher who knows how to sustain the weary is Yahweh himself. He is the one to give the right words to speak.

To have a disciple's tongue implies that, as a matter of principle and general character, the prophet has done his learning. He has soaked himself in the words of the Torah, in the words of the prophets who lived before the exile, in the words of the Psalms. We know this is the case because he often reflects their language. Isaiah of Jerusalem in particular had spoken of his own teaching being preserved among his disciples against the day when Israel would take it more seriously, and it may be significant that Isaiah of the exile here picks up the term that the first Isaiah had used. He sees himself as a disciple of the earlier prophet, called to soak himself in his teaching and become with him a disciple of Yahweh himself. He was a disciple of Yahweh in this general sense: he knew that no human message would do, and that it had to be what Yahweh taught.

Then he knew that this principle had to be applied day by

day. He has to listen morning by morning. It is not, after all, so difficult to gain a general grasp of the truth, to know the Bible fairly well, to attain a fundamentally biblical theology. But to know what in particular needs to be said on a specific occasion is a very different matter. The Bible itself manifests considerable variety. Isaiah of Jerusalem says Yahweh is committed to Jerusalem and it will not fall, Jeremiah says he is not committed to Jerusalem and it will fall. Leviticus incorporates chapter after chapter about how to offer sacrifice, Amos says Yahweh is not really interested in sacrifice. Paul says the really important thing is faith, James says the really important thing is works. At different times the people of God need different things to be said to them. Thus the servant of God needs to be not only in a general sense a disciple of the Lord, to acknowledge that the message must come from him, and to be well acquainted with the Scriptures. This principle has also to be applied from decade to decade, from year to year and from day to day. It is easy to persist in declaring what was really the Lord's word yesterday, but is inappropriate today because people are not in the same situation. As we have seen, this was characteristic of the false prophets in Israel. They were preaching yesterday's message, comforting people with words of prophecy that did not apply to them. An authentic prophet knows what Yahweh is saying today and is willing to confront people with it. A schoolboy listens to his teacher morning by morning. So it is also in Yahweh's school. The servant listens in order that he can speak.

HE IS ONE WHO ACCEPTS AFFLICTION AS THE PRICE OF MINISTRY

So 'today's' message from Yahweh to his people is one of comfort and encouragement for the exiles. The message is not as acceptable to the exiles as one might have thought. It was presumably even less acceptable to the Babylonians. Here is a prophet telling the wretched Jews that the Babylonians' enemy Cyrus is going to defeat Babylon. It will not be surprising that they feel compelled to do something about this dangerous man. So the price of being willing to bring God's word to the weary is to feel their enemies' rod on one's own back.

> *The Lord Yahweh opened my ear,*
> *and I myself did not resist,*
> *I have not turned away.*
> *I yielded my back to flogging*
> *and my chin to those who tore at my beard.*
> *I did not hide my face*
> *from insults and spitting (50:5-6).*

The servant's piety in private (50:4) is backed up by courage in public, as he has had to face the fact that (like Jeremiah's) his ministry brought trouble to the prophet himself. The picture here is reminiscent of that of Jesus, though the passage is not applied to him in the New Testament. The picture is also reminiscent of Paul. He, too, found that there was a cost involved in ministry, meeting with attack and persecution in many parts of the Mediterranean world where he was commissioned to spread the gospel (as he tells us in 2 Corinthians). He, too, accepts the affliction that comes to him, because he can see it has a positive purpose: 'I am happy about my sufferings for you, for by means of my physical sufferings I am helping to complete what still remains of Christ's sufferings on behalf of his body, the church' (Col. 1:24 GNB).

In the same way, Isaiah of the exile accepted what came to him: *I did not resist, I have not turned away. I yielded ..., I did not hide ...* He knew it was Yahweh's will. He had a disciple's tongue, he had been declaring Yahweh's word, and he could therefore take the consequences. He accepts affliction as the price of ministry. There is admittedly more to it than that, because somehow (as the story of Jeremiah hints, and as Paul recognizes) the acceptance of affliction achieves something. It speaks of the God who is willing to take pain and suffering himself, and actually helps to bridge the gulf between God and man. But that becomes more explicit in Isaiah 53.

HE IS ONE WHO REMAINS CONFIDENT OF
YAHWEH'S VINDICATION

But the Lord Yahweh will help me.
Thus I do not feel intimidated
and have set my face like flint.
I know I will not be disappointed.
My vindicator is near—who dares dispute with me?
Let us confront one another.
Who considers he has a case against me?
Let him come forward.
The Lord Yahweh will indeed help me:
what man can put me in the wrong?
They will indeed wear out like clothes,
eaten up by moths! (50:7-9).

The key factor in the situation is again Yahweh's word. It was he who gave Isaiah of the exile his message about Cyrus defeating the Babylonians. The prophet could cope with their attacks because he knew that in the end they were doomed to fail.

How will he be vindicated? Does he imagine Yahweh intervening in his trial at the hand of the Babylonians? Does he see the fulfilment of his prophecies as being his vindication? Does he hope that his sufferings will contribute to his vindication? (This is taken up in Isaiah 53). We do not know, and perhaps he did not. All he knew was that Yahweh was faithful.

We noted above a certain parallel between the experience of Paul and those of the servant prophet. Paul himself also takes up the theme of this passage and applies it to Christians generally. 'If God is for us, who can be against us? ... Who will bring a charge against those whom God has chosen? It is God who justifies. Who is going to condemn?' So nothing can separate us from God's love (Rom. 8:31-39). God's servant can always be confident of God's vindication.

THE SERVANT'S CHALLENGE

In giving his testimony, the servant has implicitly placed a choice before his hearers. Do his fellow exiles intend to walk

in the way of the servant, or in the way of his attackers? Two
alternative and contrasting positions lie before them. The
challenge becomes explicit in the verses that follow the
servant's testimony (50:10-11). In a sense these are the climax
towards which the testimony has been leading. He wants to
challenge them to walk the way of a disciple, not the way
of an oppressor. The exiles stand between these alternatives.

> *Who is there among you that fears Yahweh*
> *and listens to the voice of his servant,*
> *who walks in darkness*
> *with no light to shine for him?*
> *He must trust in Yahweh*
> *and rely on his God (50:10).*

Here the prophet is actually raising the flag for the formation
of a faithful remnant. The idea of the remnant appears in
several forms. The actual word has been used once or twice
in these chapters. It was there when the prophet spoke about
restoring the preserved of Israel, restoring what was left of
Israel (49:6). That is the most basic thing that the idea means:
the remnant is those that are lucky enough to be left alive
after Yahweh's judgement. In this sense, outwardly the
remnant is not a group that is less sinful and rebellious than
Israel in general. They are simply the ones who, by Yahweh's
grace, are allowed to escape his judgement. But that challenges them to become the remnant in the inward sense: the
responsive, faithful remnant. This is the prophet's challenge.
'You have heard me describing the life of a servant of God.
God calls you to be willing to walk that way.'

He also promises that it is the only worthwhile way,
because the alternative is to slide into the way of the
oppressor. That may be easier in the short run, but in the end
it means being consumed by the fire you light.

> *But all you who are kindling a fire*
> *and surrounding yourself with sparks,*
> *walk in the flames of your fire*
> *and among the sparks you have lit.*
> *It is by my doing that this comes to you,*
> *so that you will lie down in torment (50:11).*

CHAPTER TEN

The triumphant servant (Isaiah 52:13-53:12)

After the challenge to respond to the servant's testimony
(50:10), the servant motif disappears for a while (51:1
-52:11). The prophet continues to encourage the exiles' faith,
both directly and indirectly (by exhorting Yahweh himself to
act, as in 51:9-11).

When the servant motif reappears (52:13 - 53:12: I refer to
this passage loosely as 'Isaiah 53') it is developed quite mar-
kedly. Themes that have been present earlier are taken up
and taken further. The chapter as a whole is a deep and
mysterious one. It is one of the most difficult passages in the
Old Testament to translate into English (hence the differences
between the standard English translations). Many of the
Hebrew words it uses are uncommon ones, the way the words
fit together is often unclear, and (largely as a consequence of
this) scholars suspect that at various points the chapter has
been altered by scribes, accidentally or purposefully, perhaps
as a result of their own difficulty in understanding it. And yet
it may be strangely appropriate that this deep and mysterious
portrait of the suffering servant should be puzzling in many
of its details. This helps to ensure that we do not make the
mistake of thinking that we have totally grasped the picture it
presents to us.

Indeed, I think 'picture' or 'vision' is the most helpful way to look at this chapter. We are familiar with visions related by Old Testament prophets. As we noted in chapter 3, Jeremiah once 'saw' the world devastated as by a nuclear holocaust, a vision which spoke of the destruction hanging over Judah (see Jer. 4:23-28). Ezekiel relates a whole series of visions relating to the fall of Jerusalem and the coming restoration. In the New Testament, the book of Revelation presents itself substantially as one long vision (see Rev. 4:1). Again, some Christians today believe that they are sometimes given a 'picture' which expresses a message from God (it is interesting that, in my experience, they avoid the word 'vision'—but the phenomenon is very similar). Our dreams, too, even if they are not supposed to have any religious significance, characteristically consist of a bewildering amalgam of images and memories from what has happened to us recently (or long ago) and from what has been on our minds.

So what the prophet is relating to us is a vision or a picture which has come to him and which addresses (sometimes obliquely, sometimes directly) the concerns of his own ministry among the exiles, and reflects in different ways his own experience with the exiles and his subliminal acquaintance with various features of Israelite religion. This varied experience and knowledge contributes a range of motifs and images which combine together to form something quite new and revolutionary, in the picture of a man afflicted but righteous, concerned to bring *shalom* to others and suffering for that, but ultimately triumphant and fruitful.

WHAT THE PROPHET ACTUALLY SEES

Isaiah of the exile pictures a man. He is not at all impressive.

He grew straight up like a young plant
with its roots in dry ground (53:2).

Healthy, fruitful plants, tall, strong trees, and beautiful, flourishing flowers grow only in well-watered ground. 'A tree planted by streams of water ... yields its fruit in its season, its leaf does not wither' (Ps. 1:3). But the Israelite was familiar with the fact that as one travels south in his country, the land becomes drier and dustier and the trees become scarcer and more straggly, because they grow out of dry ground.

People, too, can be like that. This is true physically, as the pictures we see of undernourished children from starvation areas remind us. But it is also true psychologically. People who have not been nourished emotionally or intellectually tend to grow up with their development of spirit, feelings or mind stunted. They are like plants with their roots in dry ground. This servant, too, reminded you of someone whose growth had been stunted.

Consequently there was nothing impressive or handsome about him. Nothing drew your attention to him. Now Jews do not have the negative attitude to physical appearances and material blessings which has often characterized the Church. Their positive attitude goes back to a belief in God as the creator of the world and the Lord of material things. The Old Testament assumes that although God does look on the heart, nevertheless outward appearances matter; God is interested in them, too. Thus the Israelites expected their kings, for instance, to be six feet tall and stunningly handsome—and this is how Saul and David are described. 'You are the most handsome of men', the king is told (Ps. 45:2). It is appropriate for him to be that.

But the man in the vision is not like this at all.

He had no dignity or majesty to make us look at him.
His appearance did not attract us to him (53:2).

Worse than that, he was a man *tormented by pain and humbled by suffering* (53:3). What kind of suffering? The prophet seems to refer both to physical *illness* and to persecution, and it is likely that we should not be too prosaic in utilizing every detail of the picture in order to form a composite whole—to prove he had one particular illness or had been attacked in one particular way. And yet we ought to take note of the various elements in the picture, because they all contribute to the total effect of suffering and degradation.

Suffering tends to disfigure people. So it was with the man in the vision.

> *He was disfigured, he no longer looked human.*
> *His appearance was no longer that of a man (52:14).*

Sometimes a person or a photograph in a newspaper will make us shudder, and we may hear people say that such pictures of maimed or deformed people ought not to be put in the newspapers or on television. Such was the reaction aroused by the man in the vision. People were shocked and appalled at the sight of him. He himself knew this, and had to live with it.

> *He seemed vile, and avoided people,*
> *tormented by pain and humbled by suffering,*
> *like something men turn their faces from.*
> *He seemed vile, and we took no notice of him (53:3).*

He knew what he looked like, and he knew how people felt about him, so he avoided them and thereby in a sense saved himself the pain of rejection. For if he did come into contact with people, he found that no-one would look at him or acknowledge him. He was ignored, treated as if he did not exist. They could not cope with the sight except by ignoring it.

There was once a theory that what is actually being described here is a case of leprosy. Leprosy can eat away people's limbs and features, and one reason why the human instinct is to shut lepers away is that the sight is too much for people to cope with. It was the same with lunatics in the early part of this century. It is unlikely that the prophet really has leprosy specifically in mind, but that suggestion gives the right impression: an appalling, disfiguring ailment that makes people instinctively recoil. Thus the man in the vision is without family or friends; he is alone. He is a social outcast.

That was a psychological reaction for people in the first instance. But it became a theological principle. God had told Israel that there was generally a relationship between sin and suffering. Where relationships with God were right, there would be wholeness, growth, and health. When things went wrong between man and God, one by-product would be that things went wrong in man's other relationships (with the world, with nature, with society, with other men) and within man himself. Yahweh would protect Israel from illness when things were right between her and God, but not when things were wrong.

So if they saw a man physically ill, for instance, it was at least a fair question whether things had gone wrong between him and God. The story of Job, of course, makes it clear that this is not always the explanation, and many of the Psalms testify to this, too. But people easily slipped into the equation: sickness must imply sin. So they did with the man in this vision. In a sense what they were doing was rationalizing their instinctive rejection of him. They were providing a theological excuse for making him into a social outcast. Thus

We for our part reckoned that he was afflicted,
struck down by God, and brought low (53:4).

For the man in the vision, trouble then compounded itself. If people have made up their mind that someone is suffering so awfully that he must be an appalling sinner, then they may reckon it appropriate to treat him as an appalling sinner and to infer what sins he must have committed (as Job's 'friends' did with Job). After all, the presence of sin in the community is not a mere private affair. It affects the whole people. It therefore has to be dealt with. Thus

He was arrested and sentenced, and led away.
And who gave a thought to his fate?
Yes, he was torn from the world of the living (53:8).

He was condemned by society and *counted among rebels* (53:12), included among those who threw off the laws of God and of the community. But then his status as a social outcast was reinforced and deepened. He was not even to receive an honourable burial. For an Old Testament Jew, to die was to join your ancestors. He joined them physically in the family tomb. To be deprived of that last privilege is the final indignity, the final sadness and loss.

He was given a grave among criminals,
among the lowest of men at his death (53:9).

So what one actually saw in this man was a rather pathetic, underprivileged, unimpressive person; one who was disfigured by suffering and pain in such a way that he was shunned by men in general; one who was then assumed to be a marked transgressor and was treated as such, so that eventually he paid the ultimate penalty and was denied even family burial. But there was more to him than that.

WHAT THE PROPHET'S INSIGHT PERCEIVES

There was something very puzzling about this man. The picture did not quite add up. He was thought to be a notorious sinner; that was assumed to be demonstrated by the suffering he had experienced. But when one looked at his reaction to the treatment he received when people had decided that he was a wrongdoer, it did not fit. He did not react in the way you would expect of the notorious sinner he was supposed to be.

He was harshly treated, though he submitted himself,
he did not open his mouth,
like a lamb led to the butcher's,
like a sheep dumb before her shearers.
He did not open his mouth (53:7).

Indeed, what wrong was he supposed to have done? He was *assumed* to be a gross sinner, but what was the evidence? When that question was asked, a strange contrast appeared between his fate and the life he had actually lived.

He was given a grave among criminals,
among the lowest of men at his death,
although he had done no wrong
and his mouth had uttered no lie (53:9).

So why did he suffer the way he did? If he did not suffer afflic-

tion because he deserved it, was his suffering meaningless?
Was there no explanation of it?

> Yet it was our suffering that he took,
> our pain he bore,
> whereas we had reckoned that he was afflicted,
> struck down by God, and brought low.
> But he was wounded because of our rebellion,
> crushed because of our wrongdoing (53:4-5).

(The words in roman type are emphasized in Hebrew). Why
was this good man willing to be afflicted? One reason was
that he wanted to identify with other people in their affliction.
To say he has borne our suffering does not in itself mean that
he bore it instead of us. It can just mean that he bore it with
us, when he did not have to. When a Jew 'sits shiva' with
someone, he bears their grief and carries their sorrows, in
the sense that he shares them. That is something very valuable.
One of the worst things about suffering is the feeling that you
are alone, and it is some comfort to have someone to share
your suffering with you. The man in the vision let himself be
afflicted so that he could share the affliction which people in
general brought on themselves by their sin.

But there is more to it than that. Here is this man who has
done no wrong. He is a righteous man: that is Yahweh's own
description (53:11). There was indeed a contrast between the
man and the people who were watching him. But it was not,
after all, that he was much more wicked than them. It was
that he was much more righteous than them. He set a new
standard of righteousness. After all, how many people
manage to accept unfair treatment and hostile attacks in the
way he does? How many people manage to control their
words the way he did? Much later, James was to comment on
what an uncontrollable fire the tongue is (James 3:6-9). Jesus
declared that it was really unnecessary to worry about the
kosher food laws because what actually defiles a man is not
what goes into his mouth, but what comes out of it. No-one
can be sinless as far as his words are concerned. But the man
in the vision could keep his mouth shut (53:7). 'Silence under
Suffering is a strange thing in the Old Testament—a thing

absolutely new ... In the Old Testament the sufferer is always either confessing his guilt to God, or, when he feels no guilt, challenging God in argument ... Why was this Servant the unique and solitary instance of silence under suffering?' (George Adam Smith, *The Book of Isaiah*, Volume II, 1890, pp. 359-60). Further, when he did open his mouth, he always spoke in accordance with the truth (53:9). Most strikingly, he 'made intercession for the transgressors' (53:12 RSV). There is more to this last line of the poem than that translation implies, as we shall suggest below, but the servant's attitude to those who afflict him at least includes this, that when he does open his mouth in the presence of those who are putting him to death for no reason, it is to pray for them. Who is this man?

In setting a new standard of righteousness, he makes people see themselves as sinners in a way they have not before. They started off feeling rather superior and upright when they compared themselves with him, but suddenly everything seemed to get turned upside down. As they looked more closely at him, they found that they had exchanged labels with him. He was supposed to be the sinner, they were the righteous. But as they continued to look at him, they found that he was the righteous one and they were the sinners. So he is suffering and they are not, whereas they are the sinners and he is not. Indeed *he* seems to be suffering for *their* sin, not merely in suffering alongside them, but in going through things which consequently they do not have to go through, even though he deserves those things much less than they do.

> He gave himself utterly, even to death,
> and let himself be counted among rebels.
> He took the sin of many
> and intervened for the rebels (53:12).

The point is made in a more technical way by speaking of his life as *offered for the guilt of others* (53:10). The prophet applies to him a term from the religious laws in Leviticus and Numbers, usually translated as 'guilt-offering' (see Lev. 5-6). The prophet's acquaintance with these religious laws thus contributes one of the motifs which make up the eventual complex amalgam of his picture.

Now these laws included regulations for various types of sacrifice. Not all these sacrifices were centrally concerned with the problem of human sin and the barrier between man and God. Some were simply expressions of joyful fellowship or of gratefulness for answered prayer. But then there were others that *were* concerned with the problem of human sin. Regular 'sin-offerings' (see Lev.4) dealt with accidental religious offences. On the annual Day of Atonement (see Lev.16) the wilful sins of the nation were transferred to a goat which was driven off into the wilderness. To us, such a ritual may seem only to heighten the problem: how can driving a goat into the wilderness deal with human sin? But somehow in Yahweh's providence it did. The other major kind of regular sacrifice concerned with sin was the 'guilt-offering', to which Isaiah of the exile refers here. One particular function of this rite was to make restitution in connection with deliberate crimes such as robbery. The guilty person had to restore what he had stolen, but his offence was also a 'breach of faith against Yahweh' (Lev. 6:2), and his act therefore had to be dealt with as a sin as well as a crime. The 'guilt-offering' or 'restitution-offering' was the means of getting right with Yahweh in such a situation of deliberate sin. The servant's life is offered on behalf of sinners in the way that an animal's life is offered according to this rite.

Israelite religious law had no place for human sacrifice. The Israelites were aware of this practice, but they knew it as a Canaanite one, into which Israel fell only in times of apostasy. Long before the time of Moses, their forefather Abraham had come close to offering Isaac his son as a human sacrifice to God, but he had then been told that this was not required (see Gen. 22). God valued Abraham's willingness to yield up to him the one most dear to him, the one whom God had himself designed as the means by which he was going to fulfil his promise to Abraham. But the actual doing of the act was prohibited. God provided a goat instead.

On the other hand, the possibility of one righteous man giving his life to secure the lives of a sinful people had been raised before in Israel's history. We referred in chapter 2 to Moses' offer to give his life for the lives of Israel when the

Israelites had made the golden calf and Yahweh's anger burnt hot against them (see Exod. 32:30-32). Yahweh does not allow Moses to bear the people's sin in this way, but the idea of one man dying for the sins of people is there. Again, in the opening chapter of Deuteronomy, Moses speaks of himself as forbidden to enter the promised land because of Yahweh's anger, not with him but with the Israelite people (Deut. 1:37). Moses offering to be punished and actually being punished for the sins of the people; here is another thread in the tapestry that the prophet is weaving. The servant is, in a sense, a new Moses, one who will really do what Moses wanted to do on the people's behalf. He is thus not a dumb animal, led to the butcher's uncomplaining because it does not recognize the place (53:7). He is not even, like Isaac, led off to Mount Moriah to be offered to God because his father thinks it is a good idea. Like Moses, the man in the vision offers himself. As a mature adult he faces up to the need of a sacrifice, and agrees to be the sacrifice.

The necessity of sacrifice presupposes the breakdown of relationship between man and God. The achievement of the servant's affliction is to restore that relationship, and to restore the wholeness which depends upon it.

The chastening that brings us 'shalom' was required of him and through his wounds healing came to us (53:5).

Some time ago the prophet lamented Israel's loss of *shalom* and declared that rebels (like her) could never find it again (48: 18, 22). It is rediscovered through someone being chastened on her behalf. Way back at the beginning of the book of Isaiah, Israel is a sick man, bruised and beaten because of his rebelliousness (1:5-6). Healing comes through someone being wounded on his behalf.

The servant willingly accepted what came to him for the sake of these who needed to be brought back to God. But the prophet perceives also that Yahweh himself was involved. *Yahweh has brought down on him the guilt that belonged to all of us (53:6).* Yahweh was involved in the career of his anointed, Cyrus, through whom Israel was to be brought back to Palestine, and had said about him, *he will fulfil my whole plan* (44:28). He is involved also in the career (or the anti-career) of his unnamed servant, through whom wholeness is to be restored to all those who acknowledge him, and the prophet says about him, *it was Yahweh's plan to crush him with pain* (53:10). As in the case of Cyrus, this involves no overriding of the human will: the one through whom he works willingly accepts the role of Yahweh has in mind for him, and thereby his will and Yahweh's will co-incide.

His life thus reveals something of Yahweh's own power. This is where the witnesses' testimony began.

> *Who would have believed what we have heard?*
> *To whom has Yahweh's power manifested itself? (53:1).*

We are familiar with the idea of the power of Yahweh (more literally, the 'arm' of Yahweh). What it suggests is made clear only a few verses before this vision of the suffering servant: 'Yahweh has bared his holy arm before the eyes of all the nations, and all the ends of the earth will see our God act to save us' (52:10). Yahweh's arm raised in violent action against his enemies is a characteristic Old Testament motif. But here in the vision of the servant is a very different understanding of the arm of Yahweh. 'Who could have seen the LORD's hand in this' (53:1 GNB): in the affliction and humiliation of his servant? Strange power of God, manifested in such weakness.

Thus the prophet's insight perceives that the man who was afflicted did not behave like a wrongdoer. So why was he suffering? To share the experience of those who do suffer. But then when he looks at him more closely he sees that he is afflicted more severely than others, even though he deserves it much less than others (in fact, not at all). One look at the servant makes it clear that they are the sinners, not he. He is in fact suffering in their place, in the way that an animal does when it is offered in sacrifice. And the whole thing is somehow Yahweh's own idea, and its reveals something very deep about him and about where his real might lies.

WHAT THE PROPHET ULTIMATELY LOOKS FOR

The servant *gave himself utterly, even to death* (53:12). So is there any future for him?

> *When his life is offered for the guilt of others,*
> *He will see his offspring and enjoy long life (53:10).*

His suffering is not to be the end of him. He is to enjoy a full life, despite the death he seems to have died. What does an Old Testament believer look for from a full life? He hopes to beget many sons, so that his quiver is full of them (Ps. 127:5), and to live to a good old age, be full of years (Gen. 25:8). Despite what he has been through, *he will see his offspring and enjoy long life*, the witnesses declare. He was involved in Yahweh's purpose, and Yahweh will see justice is done.

But one doubts if a man like this was very concerned for his own future. He had surrendered himself to the needs of sinful man and to the purpose of Yahweh. His concern will be, what about those needs? What about that purpose? He is promised that the purpose will be achieved and the needs will be met. It will not all be useless.

> *Through him Yahweh's purpose will prosper.*
> *He will see fruit from his deep affliction,*
> *He will find satisfaction through his humiliation.*
> *My servant, being righteous, will bring righteousness to*
>   *many.*
> *He will bear their guilt himself (53:10-11).*

Early on in the exposition of the servant motif, the servant's concern for bringing God's just judgement to the weak and needy emerged as a significant feature in his calling (see 42:1-4); he is involved in Yahweh's righteous purpose (42:6). The servant is now promised the satisfaction of knowing that his affliction does not ruin that purpose: his humiliation bears fruit in bringing righteousness to many. At the beginning of the poem Yahweh promises,

> *My servant will succeed (52:13).*

At the end, Yahweh promises that his achievement will be acknowledged and rewarded.

I will give him many as his possession
and he will distribute the mighty as spoil (53:12).

Indeed, the way his success is to be acknowledged perhaps implies something more than the honour of a great man.

He will rise to greatness and high honour (52:13).

The words recall those of Isaiah of Jerusalem at the beginning of his ministry, when he saw his vision of Yahweh the holy one in his temple, 'high and exalted' (Isa. 6:1). It is the same words that are used of the servant in this vision near the end of the book of Isaiah. He receives 'a share in the dignity of Yahweh himself' (D.R. Jones, in *Peake's Commentary on the Bible*, 1962, p.527). Mysteriously the power of God was manifested in his humiliation (53:1), and mysteriously the glory of God is reflected in his triumph.

Thus, whereas people have been appalled at the sight of the servant in his disfigurement, now they will rise to their feet to acknowledge him in his triumph. Whereas people once derided him, then they will be speechless at the sight of him in his moment of success. Then they will acknowledge that they have seen something quite unprecedented and unique, something they had never dreamt of, something no-one could have believed or seen the significance of. But they will at last perceive it.

He will bring many nations to their feet
and kings will stand speechless before him,
because they have seen something they have not been told
  before,
and contemplated something they have not heard of before
  (52:15).

What the prophet ultimately looks for is the servant's vindication. He seems to be finished, but he will live a long and happy life yet. His suffering was not pointless; it will bring release to many. His humiliation was not permanent; he will receive a share in the exaltation of God himself. He will not be despised for ever, but acknowledged by nations and kings. Ordinary sight sees only the affliction. But the eyes of faith see the meaning behind it, and the eyes of hope see the fruit that is to issue from it.

WHO IS THIS MAN?

I noted at the beginning of the chapter that many of the details of the prophet's portrayal of the servant in Isaiah 53 are difficult to interpret, though the overall picture is clear enough. Its biggest mystery, however, is the question, who is this servant in the prophet's vision?

What might the prophet himself have answered if we had been able to ask him the question? I suspect his first response would have been to say, 'Well, I have told you all I know. It is there in the book. I have nothing else to tell you. If I had, I would have put it in.'

But then if we pressed him with the question, 'How is the vision going to come true?', there are two things he *might* have said. One is this. 'I have been describing to you, or expressing in this vision, certain insights that I have come to about how God is going to bring Israel back to himself, and how he is going to bring light to the world. I know from the Torah, for instance, that God speaks of sacrifice being necessary if sin is to be atoned for. I know from what Israel has gone through and from what Yahweh has promised with regard to her future, that it is possible for affliction to be followed by triumph and for death to be followed by resurrection. I know from my own experience as a prophet that bringing people back to God often demands a personal cost, a personal self-giving, a personal dying on the part of the one who is involved in ministry. So in a sense what I have been describing in this vision is what needs to happen if the deepest problem between man and God is to be dealt with. I do not know how it is going to be achieved. But that is what does need to be achieved.'

'But that is really too tentative a way to put it. It might

suggest that I am only saying what needs to happen, but have no conviction that it ever will happen. That is not what I mean. God gave me my vision. It is about his purpose for the world. It is about what he promises he is going to do. So it is not just my pious hope. It is God's promise. But how he is going to keep his promise—well, I do not know about that.'

So has the vision found its realization? Jewish interpretation of Isaiah 53 has naturally been struck by the parallels between the portrait of the servant and the experience of the Jewish people. Indeed, Isaiah of Jerusalem himself described the suffering of Israel (more accurately, of Judah) in these terms, in a passage referred to above.

> *Your head is covered with sores,*
> *your body diseased;*
> *from head to foot there is not a sound spot in you -*
> *nothing but bruises and weals and raw wounds*
> *which have not felt compress or bandage*
> *or soothing oil*

Isaiah goes on to make it quite clear that the portrait of the sick man is a metaphorical description of the nation:

> *Your country is desolate, your cities lie in ashes.*
> *Strangers devour your land before your eyes ...*
> *(1:5-7 NEB).*

That earlier passage from Isaiah at least makes it clear that the fact that the picture in Isaiah 53 is clearly a picture of an individual man does not mean that the servant referred to needs be one man - the Messiah to come, or the prophet himself, or a contemporary such as the exiled and imprisoned King Jehoiachin (though the suffering of the prophet and that of the king in exile may have contributed to the picture). The nation as a whole is like a sick man, who eventually (with the exile) actually dies. But death need not be the end. 'Can these bones live again?', Yahweh asks Ezekiel. Ezekiel wisely declines to express on opinion, but Yahweh says to the bones, 'I will put muscles on you, I will bring flesh on you, I will cover you with skin, and I will put breath in you, and you will come to life' (Ezek. 37:3-6). Israel before the exile was a sick man and Israel in the exile is a corpse, but Yahweh promises he can restore her to life.

Often since that time Israel has suffered in the way the servant did. Often her suffering has been relatively undeserved. Sometimes her suffering has borne fruit for others: the death of the six million might make it unlikely that the world will tolerate another Hitler (as D.N. Freedman suggests in an article on 'The biblical idea of history' in *Interpretation* 21, 1967, p. 48). The trouble is, however, that the world has a short memory. Again, would the State of Israel have been founded except for the West's need to salve its conscience for the holocaust? The trouble is, however, that even the State of Israel may not be safe. The Jewish novelist Saul Bellow relates in his diary of a four month stay in Israel, *To Jerusalem and Back* (1976) (p.15), 'A Jewish professor at Harvard recently said to me, "Wouldn't it be the most horrible of ironies if the Jews had collected themselves conveniently in one country for a second holocaust?" '.

Israel's own story does illustrate aspects of the vision of the suffering servant. But in other respects it does not quite fit. We have already seen that in the prophet's view Israel as much as the nations is rebellious instead of righteous, and herself needs to find *shalom*. Like the church, she needs the ministry of the servant, who is (unlike her) righteous, uncomplaining, unvengeful, undeceiving, praying for his persecutors, before she can function as God's servant herself. The actual text of the passage seems to make explicit that the servant and the people are to be distinguished, by drawing a comparison between their sufferings:

As many were appalled by you (my people, NEB adds), so he was disfigured ... (52:14).

But certainly Israel's suffering contributes something to the prophet's vision; to be the servant is Israel's calling, to suffer like the servant has been her experience, and it is in some ways distasteful for a gentile to refuse to allow her to find herself in this passage.

Nevertheless the Christian's testimony is that there is one

particular Jew who has lived up to the portrait offered by the
vision of Isaiah 53, and that is Jesus of Nazareth. The New
Testament picks up many of the specific phrases of the
chapter to apply them to Jesus. His life manifested no sin or
untruth (1 Peter 2:22, compare Isa. 53:9). His ministry took
many people's suffering and pain (Matt. 8:17, compare Isa.
53:4). His mission met with disbelief (John 12:37-38, compare
Isa. 53:4). He accepted oppression without protest (Acts 8:
32-33, compare Isa. 53:7-8). He let himself be taken as a
criminal (Luke 22:37, compare Isa. 53:12). He died to bear
men's sins, to heal men's wounds, to restore straying sheep to
their shepherd (1 Peter 2:24-25, compare Isa. 53:5-6). The
conviction that Jesus fulfils the vision of the servant of
Yahweh lies behind other passages where reference to Isaiah
53 is more allusive:

> Of his own free will he gave up all he had,
> and took the nature of a servant ...
> He was humble and walked the path of obedience
>   all the way to death -
> his death on the cross.
> For this reason God raised him to the highest place above
> and gave him the name that is greater than any other name
> ... (Phil. 2:7-9 GNB)

Jesus is the suffering and triumphant servant par excellence.

To see Jesus as the fulfilment of this vision in Isaiah 53
brings home to us two aspects of his ministry. One is that he
suffers to effect atonement between God and man. 'God was
in Christ ...'; the suffering of Jesus is the suffering of the
crucified God himself, letting men do their worst to him so
that he can make an end to their sin once and for all by
absorbing all the hostility and aggression they can express.
Man's fundamental problem is his sin; the starting-point of
Jesus' proclamation is his very Jewish call for repentance or
turning from sin (Mark 1:15), and the culmination of his
work is his dying for sin.

But often man's felt problem is not his sin but his pain and
his suffering; and what often actually drew people to Jesus
was his concern for and his ability to deal with such needs.
The church has been experiencing a new realization of this in

the widespread concern with healing - indeed, there is once again a danger of a loss of perspective, of forgetting that sin and atonement remain the fundamental matters. But as long as we see that our need of forgiveness remains our deepest need, we can go on to rejoice that because Jesus died for us the rest of our ills can be dealt with precisely because sin, atonement, and forgiveness are the root matters. We can bring our sins to the cross and leave them there; we can also bring our pains, our griefs, and our sorrows to the cross and leave them there too. We need not hang on to them. The servant suffers both for our rebellion and for our pain and suffering.

It is striking, however, that when the epistles in the New Testament speak of Jesus in these terms, the context is concerned not merely with a right understanding of Jesus, but with his followers' willingness to walk the way Jesus walked. 'Christ ... left you an example, so that you might follow in his steps ...' (1 Peter 2:21); 'the attitude you should have is the one Christ Jesus had ...' (Phil. 2:5 GNB). The danger of the quest for the identity of the servant in Isaiah 53 is that it diverts us from the same challenge which this chapter lays before us. The poem offers a vision of what God wants to do and can do with someone prepared to be his servant. The poem is, to use a more prosaic term, a job-description. Or it is a challenge to the reader as to whether he is prepared to be a servant of this kind. The challenge, or invitation, may be accepted by Israel as a nation or by the church or by individuals who are willing to take it seriously. While Christians are convinced that Jesus alone met the challenge in the fullest sense, this does not mean that the passage is now a dead thing from the past, relevant only as a promise fulfilled in Christ. It is still God's vision for his people, and God's challenge to them.

The poem ... exists to create another world, a world indeed that is recognizably our own, with brutality and suffering and God and a coming-to-see on the part of some, but not a world that simply once existed and is gone for good ....
The poem can become true in a variety of circumstances ...
The world which the poem creates is a topsy-turvy world

when judged by ordinary human standards ... The social order, the strength of numbers, good taste, ordinary human decency, and the justice of God are all in turn called into question by this topsy-turvy, not to say shocking, poem. This is the world that the reader is bidden to give his assent to - or rather, to enter. It is not an obviously appealing invitation (D.J.A. Clines, *I, He, We, and They: A Literary Approach to Isaiah 53*, Journal for the Study of the Old Testament Supplement 1, 1976, pp. 61-2).

So the vision challenges us, too, as to whether we are prepared to look at our ministry the way this passage looks at the servant's. Consider what is involved. All one can actually see is disfigurement, suffering, pain, loss, abandonment, misunderstanding, and death. That is all this is visible. But then we are challenged to look with the insight of faith and see that the suffering, the pain, and the loss can be mysteriously meaningful and mysteriously glorious. But one cannot physically see this. One can see it only with the eyes of faith. We are further challenged to look with the foresight of hope, and see that the abandonment, misunderstanding and death will not be final; they will yet bear fruit and bring freedom to people. But one cannot see it now. One can see it only with the eyes of hope. That is the vision's challenge to our lives and our ministry.

The force of the poem is not simply to invite the reader to approximate his behaviour and lifestyle to that of the servant as best he can; it is rather that the figure of the servant seizes, imposes itself upon a reader ... The assumption of the servant's role becomes, not the voluntary act of a dramatic role-playing, but a compulsion by the figure of the servant (Clines, p.64).

That being the case, what I want to leave the reader with is not my reflections on the suffering servant, but the suffering servant himself. Arguably, the place for the 'text' in a sermon is not the beginning (after which it can be abandoned for the preacher's own thoughts) but the end, after it has been, one hopes, a little elucidated. (I owe this point to a paper by

David Clines, 'Notes for an Old Testament hermeneutic',
Theology, News and Notes 21, 1975, p.10). So what does
Isaiah 53 do to you?

My servant will succeed,
he will rise to greatness and high honour.
As many were appalled at you,
so he was disfigured, he no longer looked human.
His appearance was no longer that of a man.
So he will bring many nations to their feet
and kings will stand speechless before him,
because they have seen something they have not been
    told before,
and contemplated something they have not heard of
    before.
Who would have believed what we have heard?
To whom has Yahweh's power manifested itself?
He grew straight up like a young plant
with its roots in dry ground.
He had no dignity or majesty to make us look at him.
His appearance did not attract us to him.
He seemed vile, and avoided people,
tormented by pain and humbled by suffering,
like something men turn their faces from.
He seemed vile, and we took no notice of him.
Yet it was our suffering that he took,
our pain he bore,
whereas we for our part reckoned that he was afflicted,
struck down by God, and brought low.
But he was wounded because of our rebellion,
crushed because of our wrongdoing.
The chastening that brings us 'shalom' was required of
    him
and through his wounds healing came to us.
All of us have strayed like sheep,
we have each of us taken his own way,
but Yahweh has brought down on him
the guilt that belonged to all of us.
He was harshly treated, though he submitted humbly,
he did not open his mouth,
like a lamb led to the butcher's,
like a sheep dumb before her shearers.
He did not open his mouth.

He was arrested and sentenced, and led away,
and who gave a thought to his fate?
Yes, he was torn from the world of the living
because of the rebellion of my people, who deserved the
  affliction.
He was given a grave among criminals,
among the lowest of men at his death,
although he had done no wrong,
and his mouth had uttered no lie.
But it was Yahweh's plan to crush him with pain.
When his life is offered for the guilt of others,
he will see his offspring and enjoy long life
and through him Yahweh's plan will prosper.
He will see fruit from his deep affliction,
he will find satisfaction through his humiliation.
My servant, being righteous, will bring righteousness to
  many,
he will bear their guilt himself.
Therefore I will give him many as his possession
and he will distribute the mighty as spoil,
because he gave himself utterly, even to death,
and let himself be counted among rebels.
He took the sin of many
and intervened for the rebels.

If you have ears to hear, then hear.

Index of passages
in Isaiah 40-55 and Jeremiah